"I am inspired by this compilation of nuggets cor
They are alive, wise, and relevant today as on the c   ...ank
the editor for creating this fresh resource that con\   ... ur NVC through
the inimitable way Marshall would present the teacnings—with creativity, courage,
warmth, and humor."

—**LUCY LEU**, dedicated NVC practitioner and editor of *Nonviolent Communication*

"These quotes so beautifully and powerfully capture this remarkable man who
somehow was able to create Nonviolent Communication. For over four decades, he
continuously traveled the world, tirelessly giving this incredible gift in a way that was
nothing short of magical. To be in a workshop with Marshall was to be not just deeply
moved and inspired but transported to a realm of reality that the mystics and poets
point to, and yet a place so practical, simple, and ordinary in its beauty."

—**JOHN KINYON**, CNVC trainer, mediator, and cocreator of
Mediate Your Life training based in NVC

"What a gem of a book! This is the book I would have been thrilled to have at my
fingertips after being introduced to Nonviolent Communication. I could never write
fast enough to capture Marshall Rosenberg's insightful and stirring words when
hearing him speak. For instance, 'Enemy images are the main reason conflicts don't
get resolved.' Marshall routinely interrupted audience's habitual ways of perceiving
and understanding while generating fresh insights that had the power to nourish
and heal. This timely book gathers the wisdom from Marshall's countless talks and
writings into one volume where the love and compassion of a much beloved teacher
can be richly savored. A book to help us remember and honor a man who possessed
a profound understanding of human nature and a compelling vision of how humans
are meant to live . . . in relationship with each other and with life."

—**RACHELLE LAMB**, NVC trainer and coach

"Inspired by a compassionate world that he believed was possible, Marshall Rosenberg
relentlessly pursued his vision by traveling the world multiple times over the course of
four decades.

"With a flair for engaging, entertaining, and enthralling listeners, he turned
his teaching into an artform that left lifelong impressions on many who met him.
Marshall's use of puppets, role-plays, and self-deprecating humor made it easier for us
to face difficult and painful situations, and ultimately to transform them through the
power of Nonviolent Communication."

—**JEFF BROWN**, Executive Director, Center for Nonviolent Communication

"What a wonderful and fun way to learn more about Nonviolent Communication and be inspired each day! Like meeting old and new friends, in these quotes, I am repeatedly moved by Marshall's insight, experience, passion, and humanity—as well as his playful humor. Thank you Puddle Dancer press for this treasure trove of love for humanity. This book gives me hope and direction: qualities much needed in the world today."

—DIAN KILLIAN, author of *Connecting Across Differences* and founder/director of Work Collaboratively

"This book is an absolute gem!

"Marshall's voice is loud and clear. Organized by topics, this book offers us a way into the heart of Marshall's teachings.

"It dispels any doubt about NVC being a way of life, more than a system of communication. And it clarifies that NVC is a spirituality that inclines toward social change for the benefit of all.

"Brilliant."

—STEPHANIE BACHMANN MATTEI, coauthor of *The Heart of Nonviolent Communication*, certified trainer and assessor with CNVC, and certified teacher in Mindfulness-Based Stress Reduction

"What a treasured resource this is! I love the ease and clarity of how this book organizes Marshall's life-affirming ideas. Now, rather than scouring the internet for that 'just right' quote to support my NVC training and practice, I can easily find just what I'm looking for in one place!"

—JIM MANSKE, author of *Pathways to Nonviolent Communication* and certified trainer and assessor with CNVC

"This extraordinary book from PuddleDancer Press encapsulates the wisdom from a humble guru, a man so wise that he presented himself off the pedestal, never needed to feel above anyone or anything, and who gave the world an invaluable, precious gem called NVC."

—ALAN RAFAEL SEID, CNVC certified trainer and founder of Kalapa, a school for Changemakers

"For those of us fortunate enough to have spent time in person with Marshall reading through these quotes will likely, I think, rekindle the joy we experienced. For those who didn't have that opportunity, I expect that immersing oneself in these passages—and other written and recorded materials of Marshall's—is likely to dissolve much of the social conditioning that has left so many people with so much unnecessary suffering and to connect them to a new sense of freedom and a joyful way of living.

"Even those with considerable NVC experience are likely to find gems here that they had not previously heard or read by Marshall."

—GARY BARAN, former executive director of, and certified trainer with, the Center for Nonviolent Communication, and professor emeritus of philosophy

THE
Nonviolent
COMMUNICATION
BOOK OF QUOTES

MARSHALL B. ROSENBERG, PHD

Compiled by Julie Stiles, Editor

PuddleDancer
P R E S S

2240 Encinitas Blvd., Ste. D-911, Encinitas, CA 92024
email@PuddleDancer.com • www.PuddleDancer.com

The Nonviolent Communication Book of Quotes
by Marshall B. Rosenberg, PhD

PuddleDancer Press, Permissions Dept.
2240 Encinitas Blvd., Ste. D-911, Encinitas, CA 92024
Tel: 1-760-557-0326, Email@PuddleDancer.com
www.NonviolentCommunication.com

Ordering Information
Please contact Independent Publishers Group, Tel: 312-337-0747; Fax: 312-337-5985; Email: frontdesk@ipgbook.com, or visit www.IPGbook.com for other contact information and details about ordering online.

Author: Marshall B. Rosenberg, PhD
Editor: Julie Stiles
Copyeditor: Virginia Herrick
Cover and interior design: Shannon Bodie (BookWiseDesign.com)

Manufactured in the United States of America
1st Printing, September 2023

27 26 25 24 23   1 2 3 4 5

ISBN: 978-1-934336-46-5 (trade paperback), 978-1-934336-47-2 (ebook)

Library of Congress Cataloguing-in-Publication Data

Names: Rosenberg, Marshall B., author. | Stiles, Julie, editor.
Title: The nonviolent communication book of quotes / by Marshall B. Rosenberg ; compiled by Julie Stiles.
Description: Encinitas, CA : PuddleDancer Press, [2023] | Includes bibliographical references. | Summary: "A comprehensive collection, The Nonviolent Communication Book of Quotes by NVC founder Marshall B. Rosenberg draws not only from other books and interviews, but also from the internet and previously unpublished workshops. It illuminates his revolutionary four-part Nonviolent Communication (NVC) process and shows the myriad ways NVC makes life more wonderful through the joy of compassionate giving. This essential compilation invites us to transform our lives, our work, our world" — Provided by publisher.
Identifiers: LCCN 2022051329 (print) | LCCN 2022051330 (ebook) | ISBN 9781934336465 (trade paperback) | ISBN 9781934336472 (ebook)
Subjects: LCSH: Rosenberg, Marshall B. — Quotations. | Interpersonal communication — Quotations, maxims, etc. | Interpersonal relations — Quotations, maxims, etc. | Nonviolence — Quotations, maxims, etc.
Classification: LCC BF637.C45 R647 2023 (print) | LCC BF637.C45 (ebook) | DDC 153.6 — dc23/eng20230119
LC record available at https://lccn.loc.gov/2022051329
LC ebook record available at https://lccn.loc.gov/2022051330

Thank you to
Marshall Rosenberg for making
our lives, and those of so many
others, more wonderful.

PUDDLEDANCER PRESS

CONTENTS

FOREWORD

My experience in reading *The Nonviolent Communication Book of Quotes* was at first overwhelming! I was torn, sad, inspired, and moved. Several times I had to stop reading and give self-empathy, allowing some time to process what I was feeling and needing. I was surprised by these strong emotions. I wasn't ready for them and didn't, initially, want to address them. However, as I continued to read, my chills were replaced with feelings of warmth, tenderness, delight, sweet pain, truth, honesty, and a deep connection to my beloved Marshall's presence.

This book allowed me to relive the adventurous life I shared with Marshall as he tirelessly spread his work throughout the world. It captures the essence of Marshall's spirit and his exuberant presence. I could feel, see, and hear his powerful voice, the sound of his guitar, his singing, his laughter—as he shared Nonviolent Communication with everyone he touched!

The sequence of the chapters makes the book come alive with depth, perception, and consciousness of how we choose to live and use our words. The progression connects us to our hearts and provides healthier ways to support and unite us with love and peace for the highest harmony of all concerned. The chapters flow with such grace, elegance, and a charismatic power that they brought many tears and smiles to my heart. The empowerment of my beloved Marshall's presence in the book recaptured the essence of my "aliveness," so deeply connected to the beauty of my feelings and needs.

When I was traveling with Marshall, I had the joy of seeing hundreds of people from around the world hear about Nonviolent Communication for the first time. I saw their faces light up and sparkle with such a calm, curious energy, which I now recognize as the same "aliveness" I was feeling and sensing as I finished the last few pages of this timely, valuable book.

Most importantly, these words can inspire hope, courage, awareness, and ease for us to cocreate and practice new ways to support one another as we continue to live with COVID, war, discrimination, climate change, hate, hunger, uncertainty, and so on. My beloved Marshall's words can empower us to live life with love, care, compassion, peace, honesty, passion, meaningful purpose, gratitude, humor, and respect! I can imagine this book will motivate us to focus on moving through life with grace and strength, learning to celebrate life with gusto, kindness, curiosity, and joy, and connecting us to our hearts and spirits with divine peace and love in action.

My deep gratitude to all at PuddleDancer Press who helped cocreate this dynamic, transformative collection of Marshall's words. I am deeply touched by your work to bring together the consciousness, the dedication, and the authenticity of Marshall's words into a singular resource honoring and acknowledging his tireless passion, spirit, clarity, compassion, and grace—all that makes *The Nonviolent Communication Book of Quotes* possible and alive! This book has the power to uplift our spirits and to remind us to stay connected to the precious meaning and purpose of our lives.

—VALENTINA D. ROSENBERG

PREFACE

Nonviolent Communication (NVC) began with one man's quest to find new ways of communicating that would provide peaceful alternatives to the violence he saw growing up. That man was Marshall Rosenberg. From his life experience—including a doctorate in clinical psychology and work with Carl Rogers, one of the founders of psychological research, plus study of comparative religion—Rosenberg developed the NVC process starting in the 1960s.

Over the next fifty years, Rosenberg would use this process in a variety of settings, from school integration projects to peace programs in war-torn areas of the world. He would go on to train tens of thousands of people in over sixty countries worldwide, impacting all areas of people's lives and reaching people in all types of professions and circumstances. In the 1980s, he founded the Center for Nonviolent Communication and served as its Director for Educational Services for decades, creating a certified trainer program, which now has six hundred fifty CNVC certified trainers over six continents.

With decades of writing and teaching about the principles and application of Nonviolent Communication, Marshall's direct, intimate, humorous, and powerful style affected thousands of people around the world, through countless workshops and his fifteen published books. This book pulls together under one cover, for the first time, direct quotes from all aspects of his life work.

While many people have read one or more of the books, Rosenberg's workshops reached fewer people, though they had a profound impact on those who attended. Collating the nuggets in this book brings his wisdom in both mediums—teaching and writing—to more people. Through this book, we also hope to share the meaning of Nonviolent Communication directly with the vivid, engaging, sincere, playful words of Marshall himself, whether you are new to NVC or a long-time student or practitioner.

This book was pulled together by going through all of Rosenberg's books for sections that felt particularly relevant and striking, and by finding workshop material that stood out due to its relevance and "quotability." Quotes were organized by topic and then further within each topic. For easy reference, we have added superscript numbers after each quote in this book. These numbers refer to the sources in the Works Cited (on page 273).

How to Use This Book

If you are new to Nonviolent Communication, reading through this book in the order it is laid out will give you a good overview of Rosenberg's body of work, in his own words. While we still recommend that you read *Nonviolent Communication: A Language of Life*, 3rd Edition, for a solid grounding, this book will be an excellent companion to enhance your understanding.

It begins with the basics of Nonviolent Communication—what it is, the underlying attitude of giving from the heart, and its four foundational components: observations, feelings, needs, and requests. Since Nonviolent Communication is as much (or even more) about intention as it is about technique, the next chapter covers the consciousness of Nonviolent Communication. A number of chapters then go into its more philosophical aspects, including the power of cultural conditioning, how attitudes of judgment and right/wrong get in the way, and the relationship between language and violence.

From there, the book turns to quotes about the fundamental concepts of empathy and expression. Following this foundational material are a huge variety of applications of Nonviolent Communication in different areas of life.

As with any body of work, there are words and phrases that are specific to the culture and thinking of Nonviolent Communication, a sort of "internal language" that, once you understand it, provides a shorthand to the concepts being addressed. We have regularized the style of such terms in this book. If you're an experienced practitioner, you may have seen them styled in various ways in other places. If you are new to Nonviolent Communication, you may not be familiar with them at all. But rest assured, we've chosen quotes that explain these terms, sometimes across multiple quotes, so you will understand them, as well as how and why Marshall chose to use them. These NVC-specific terms include: divine energy; domination system or domination; enemy images; giraffe; jackal; life-enriching or life-enriching system; Life Enriching Education; power-over and power-with; self-empathy; self-full and self-full-ness; and street giraffe.

If you are familiar with Nonviolent Communication, you might see this as a refresher and choose to read straight through or skip around to topics that are of particular interest to you. This can be an additional resource to further your understanding of Marshall's thinking on a variety of topics and how to apply Nonviolent Communication across all areas of your life. As you grow in your understanding, returning again and again to this book will allow new insights and realizations to emerge.

Whether you had the privilege of experiencing the power of Rosenberg's teaching in person or not, we hope that this book will inspire and strengthen you as you navigate our ever-changing, increasingly complex world.

—JULIE STILES, EDITOR

PART I

THE FOUNDATIONS OF NONVIOLENT COMMUNICATION

This process is all about compassionate giving and receiving.[21]

1

WHAT IS NONVIOLENT COMMUNICATION?

NONVIOLENT COMMUNICATION IN its purity is the most powerful, quickest way I've found to get people to go from life-alienated ways of thinking where they want to hurt each other, to enjoying giving to each other.[6]

GIVING OF OURSELVES means an honest expression of what is alive in us in this moment. . . . And the other way we give of ourselves is through how we receive another person's message. To receive it empathetically, connecting with what's alive in them, making no judgment. Just to hear what is alive in the other person and what they would like. So Nonviolent Communication is just a manifestation of what I understand love to be.[6]

THIS PROCESS IS all about compassionate giving and receiving—what I think we need to know how to do real well, if we want to enjoy being around human beings. We need to know how to connect in a way in which compassionate giving and receiving can take place.[21]

" In our training
we want people not only to
come out with awareness of how
Nonviolent Communication can be
used to transform our inner world,
we want people to see how it can
be used to create the world
outside that we want
to live in. [8] "

GENUINE COOPERATION IS inspired when participants trust that their own needs and values will be respectfully addressed. The Nonviolent Communication process is based on respectful practices that foster genuine cooperation. [11]

⤺

NONVIOLENT COMMUNICATION IS really an integration of a certain spirituality with concrete tools for manifesting this spirituality in our daily lives, our relationships, and our political activities. [8]

⤺

IN OUR TRAINING we want people not only to come out with awareness of how Nonviolent Communication can be used to transform our inner world, we want people to see how it can be used to create the world outside that we want to live in. [8]

⤺

NVC IS FOUNDED on language and communication skills that strengthen our ability to remain human, even under trying conditions. It contains nothing new; all that has been integrated into NVC has been known for centuries. The intent is to remind us about what we already know—about how we humans were meant to relate to one another—and to assist us in living in a way that concretely manifests this knowledge.

NVC guides us in reframing how we express ourselves and hear others. Instead of habitual, automatic reactions, our words become conscious responses based firmly on awareness of what we are perceiving, feeling, and wanting. We are led to express ourselves with honesty and clarity, while simultaneously paying others a respectful and empathic attention. In any exchange, we come to hear our own deeper needs and those of others. NVC trains us to observe carefully, and to be able to specify behaviors and conditions that are affecting us. We learn to identify and clearly articulate what we are concretely wanting in any given situation. The form is simple, yet powerfully transformative. [5]

NVC FOCUSES ATTENTION on whether people's needs are being fulfilled, and if not, what can be done to fulfill these needs. It shows us how to express ourselves in ways that increase the likelihood others will willingly contribute to our well-being. It also shows us how to receive the messages of others in ways that increase the likelihood that we will willingly contribute to their well-being. [9]

~

WHAT WE'RE REALLY aiming for here is to keep our attention connected to life moment by moment. We connect to the life that's going on in us, what our needs are at this moment, and focus our attention on the life that's going on in other people. [9]

~

PEOPLE CAN CHANGE how they think and communicate. They can treat themselves with much more respect, and they can learn from their limitations without hating themselves. We teach people how to do this. We show people a process that can help them connect with the people they're closest to in a way that can allow them to enjoy deeper intimacy, to give to one another with more enjoyment, and to not get caught up in doing things out of duty, obligation, guilt, shame, and the other things that destroy intimate relationships. [1]

~

NVC HELPS US learn how to create peace within ourselves when there's a conflict between what we do and what we wish we had done. If we're going to be violent to our self, how are we going to contribute to creating a world of peace? Peace begins within us. I'm not saying we have to get totally liberated from all of our inner, violent learning before we look outside of our self to the world, or to see how we can contribute to social change at a broader level. I'm saying we need to do these simultaneously. [8]

IN NONVIOLENT COMMUNICATION, we try to keep our attention focused by answering two critical questions: "What's alive in us?" and "What can we do to make life more wonderful?"

The first question, "What's alive in me; what's alive in you?" is a question that all over the planet people ask themselves when they get together: "How are you?"

Sadly, though most people ask the question, very few people really know how to answer it very well because we haven't been educated in a language of life. We've not really been taught to answer the question. We ask it, yes, but we don't know how to answer it. Nonviolent Communication, as we'll see, suggests how we can let people know what's alive in us. It shows us how to connect with what's alive in other people, even if they don't have words for saying it. [6]

NONVIOLENT COMMUNICATION SHOWS us a way of finding out what's alive in other people. It also shows us a way of seeing the beauty in the other person at any given moment, regardless of their behavior or language. You've seen that it requires connecting with the other person's feelings and needs at this moment. That's what's alive in them. And when we do it, we're going to hear the other person singing a very beautiful song. [8]

MY NEED IS for safety, fun, and to have distribution of resources, a sustainable life on the planet. NVC is a strategy that serves me to meet these needs. [34]

AS NVC REPLACES our old patterns of defending, withdrawing, or attacking in the face of judgment and criticism, we come to perceive ourselves and others, as well as our intentions and relationships, in a new light. Resistance, defensiveness, and violent reactions are minimized. [34]

WE ARE ENORMOUSLY powerful, we human beings. Every moment, we have this possibility to enrich life. And there's nothing, I find, that people throughout the world enjoy doing more than using this power in the service of life. [26]

ORIGINS, GOAL, AND USE OF NONVIOLENT COMMUNICATION

Where Did NVC Come From?

NVC EVOLVED OUT of an intense interest I have in two questions. First, I wanted to better understand what happens to human beings that leads some of us to behave violently and exploitatively. And secondly, I wanted to better understand what kind of education serves us in the attempt to remain compassionate—which I believe is our nature—even when others are behaving violently or exploitatively.

I've found in my exploration into these two questions that three factors are very important in understanding why some of us respond violently— and some of us compassionately—in similar situations. These three are:

1. The language that we have been educated to use.
2. How we have been taught to think and communicate.
3. The specific strategies we learned to influence ourselves and others. [9]

∽

I DECIDED TO do a different kind of research to observe the people I respected the most, who seemed the most compassionate, who seemed to enjoy giving to others. I tried to see: How were they different than the people who seemed to enjoy criticizing, blaming, and attacking others? [31]

∽

NONVIOLENT COMMUNICATION EVOLVED from my attempt to get conscious about beloved divine energy and how to connect with it. [6]

NONVIOLENT COMMUNICATION REALLY came out of my attempt to understand this concept of love and how to manifest it, how to do it. I came to the conclusion that it was not just something you feel, but it is something we manifest, something we do, something we have. And what is this manifestation? It is giving of ourselves in a certain way. [6]

↪

WHILE STUDYING THE factors that affect our ability to stay compassionate, I was struck by the crucial role of language and our use of words. I have since identified a specific approach to communicating—both speaking and listening—that leads us to give from the heart, connecting us with ourselves and with each other in a way that allows our natural compassion to flourish. I call this approach Nonviolent Communication, using the term *nonviolence* as Gandhi used it—to refer to our natural state of compassion when violence has subsided from the heart. While we may not consider the way we talk to be "violent," words often lead to hurt and pain, whether for others or ourselves. [5]

What Is the Goal of NVC?

NVC GIVES US tools and understanding to create a more peaceful state of mind. [34]

↪

NONVIOLENT COMMUNICATION IS not designed to help us get people to do what we want them to do. It's designed to create a connection that will get everybody's needs met and to get them met through what I call compassionate giving. People do things willingly because they see how it will serve life. [27]

↪

THE PURPOSE OF this process is to help us connect in a way that makes natural giving possible. [31]

" Remember that
our goal and the goal of
Nonviolent Communication
is not to get what we want,
but to make a human connection
that will result in everyone getting
their needs met. It's as simple,
and as complex, as that. [4] "

IF OUR OBJECTIVE is simply to change people's behavior or to get what we want, Nonviolent Communication is not the language for us. This is a language for those of us who want people to say yes to our requests only if they can do so willingly and compassionately. [4]

～

REMEMBER THAT OUR goal and the goal of Nonviolent Communication is not to get what we want, but to make a human connection that will result in everyone getting their needs met. It's as simple, and as complex, as that. [4]

What Is NVC Used For?

NVC CAN BE effectively applied at all levels of communication and in diverse situations: intimate relationships, families, schools, organizations and institutions, therapy and counseling, diplomatic and business negotiations, disputes and conflicts of any nature. [34]

～

SOME PEOPLE USE NVC to respond compassionately to themselves, some to create greater depth in their personal relationships, and still others to build effective relationships at work or in the political arena. Worldwide, NVC is used to mediate disputes and conflicts at all levels. [34]

SYMBOLS OF LANGUAGE: JACKAL AND GIRAFFE

I USE THE symbol of the jackal as the symbol of language that contributes to violence. For no other reason than that I like the word *jackal*; it just sounds funny to me. Jackals are not bad animals, but I use that for learning purposes: "Jackal Language." [21]

I USE A symbol of jackal ears for ears that make us receive things in a way that causes pain for ourselves. [12]

෴

THE LANGUAGE OF Nonviolent Communication is a language of the heart. It requires knowing how to speak always from your heart, and since giraffes have the largest heart of any land animal, what better name for a language of the heart than *giraffe*? [10]

෴

IF YOU WANT to make peace, this is the best technology I can suggest: giraffe ears. This is wonderful technology [*putting on headgear with giraffe ears attached*]. Because with this technology, no matter what people say to you, no matter how they speak, you can hear no criticism, you can hear no blame, you can't hear the word *no*. You can't hear silence, because with these ears on, the other person cannot *not* communicate a language of life. With these ears, you connect with what's alive in people, no matter how they speak, you see? [29]

෴

Participant. **SO HOW ABOUT** a tip for getting giraffe ears? [*laughter and applause*]

Marshall. Take some time every day to remind yourself of how you choose to live. To really, powerfully remind yourself. And if wearing giraffe ears helps you manifest how you choose to live, then you'll practice until you get good at it. But—don't do it mechanically. You need to first be conscious of how you choose to live. And then if giraffe ears are an effective strategy, you'll practice with a different energy than if it's just a technique. [12]

෴

I LIKE TO use the symbol of "Giraffe Language" for Nonviolent Communication because giraffes have the largest heart of any land animal and Nonviolent Communication is a language of the heart in the sense that, at the core of it are feelings and needs, which is the best way I've ever learned to describe what is alive in us at this moment. What is in our heart at this moment? Feelings and needs. [22]

NONVIOLENT COMMUNICATION IS a language of the heart. It requires us to go inside and say what's alive in us. Not up to our head, and saying what's right or wrong with other people for doing what they do. So it's a language of life. [21]

I USE THE word *jackal* as a symbol for language that contributes to violence on our planet. [29]

NOW WHEN I offer a beautiful gift of what's alive in me, and the other person says, "Oh, you're needy," or whatever, now I know what the problem is. The damned jackal postal delivery service has screwed up again. I sent a beautiful gift out, and they delivered a hunk of shit. [16]

GIRAFFE IS THAT language which makes it possible for us to connect with each other in a way in which we give from the heart to each other. [23]

SO I HAVE been interested in studying those people that have the ability to influence people to learn, but learning again that is motivated by this reverence for life, and not out of some coercive tactics.

And one of the things that I've found by studying such people is that they spoke a language that helps people to learn motivated by reverence for life.

As I've studied people who have this ability, I've noticed that they spoke a different language than the language that I was educated to speak. And this language that contributes to helping people learn by reverence for life, I call, officially, Nonviolent Communication. But for fun and teaching purposes I like calling it "Giraffe Language." [10]

⌇

SO GIRAFFE LANGUAGE is . . . in some respects like a compass. What does a compass do? It points the way back to where we want to be, even in stormy weather. So, to me, giraffe points me back to life. Having been taught to be up in my head and analyzing others and judging others, it says: "Wait a minute. Where's the life? What am I feeling? What am I needing? Where's the life in the other person? What are they feeling? What are they needing?" And it keeps my attention focused on life. And when I lose focus, it gets me back to life. [14]

⌇

PROBABLY ONE OF the most important things to be conscious of about a giraffe—we never do anything wrong. We never have, we never will. We do things we wouldn't have done, if we knew then what we're learning now. And the fun thing about life is that that'll always be the case. There's probably not a moment that we're ever doing anything that we would probably do if we knew now what we're going to learn later. Life is always changing. Wouldn't it be boring if we always knew the right thing to do? It'd be terribly boring. [17]

⌇

IF YOU HAVE giraffe ears on, you can't for one second imagine that you can be the source of another person's pain. You can't imagine that anybody would ever be angry with you. Or anybody would ever not want to be around you. It's just unimaginable. [22]

~

GIRAFFE IS TWO things: accurate empathy, and revealing yourself genuinely—what's alive in you in the moment. Not going off and talking about thoughts, unless the thoughts serve the life that's going on in the moment. [18]

~

SO IF I have giraffe ears on, I cannot hear silence. I cannot hear no. I am conscious that a *no* is a poor expression of a *yes*. If I have the giraffe ears on, I cannot hear any criticism. I'm aware that all criticism is simply a distortion of the person's needs. So the other person cannot *not* communicate, when I have these ears on. [19]

~

SEE, IF YOU have these [giraffe] ears on, the other person always speaks perfect Nonviolent Communication. That's one of the things that people like most about our training. It doesn't require the other person to cooperate. Because the moment you put these ears on, the other person speaks perfect Nonviolent Communication. [21]

~

WITH GIRAFFE EARS, if a person isn't saying anything to us, we try to keep hearing: what are their feelings and needs? We don't take it as defensiveness or resistance or rejection. We just try, as with any message— "What is this person feeling and needing?"—to stay connected to the life in them. [14]

NICE IS A smiling jackal. It is not giraffe. Giraffes are not nice. Giraffes strive to be nakedly honest. And sometimes being nakedly honest means screaming. "Hey, I want to be treated with more respect than that! If you've got a hang-up with me, tell me what I did and what you want, without calling me any names. Would you be willing to do that?" That's screaming in giraffe. [14]

⤳

GIRAFFES ARE NOT nice. Don't think that to be nonviolent requires you to be nice. Much of the violence in the world is created by nice people who sit back, no matter what's going on. No, no, no. Giraffe doesn't require you to be nice. It requires you to either be expressing your pain or your joy or hearing the other person's pain or joy. But if you're not in joy, then you're in pain. You let it be known. But you scream in giraffe, you don't scream criticism. You scream feelings, needs, requests. [22]

⤳

IF YOU'RE NOT really in touch with your feelings and needs, you're not in touch with life. Jackals can go through their whole life feeling kind of dead and not even know it, because lifelessness is their common state. And jackals think all of life is kind of lifeless. They're never very clear what they're feeling, what they're needing, what other people are feeling and needing. And when we get disconnected from feelings and needs, we feel lifeless. But if that's always how you've been, you don't even know there's another way. [14]

⤳

PEOPLE WHO SPEAK jackal are caught in this tragic bind that when they need nurturing the most, they use language almost guaranteed not to get it. [14]

⤳

I CAN USUALLY easily give a jackal response to almost any message. It's the giraffe ones that are a challenge for me. [22]

" If you're not really in touch
with your feelings and needs,
you're not in touch
with life. [14] "

NEVER PUT YOUR *but* in the face of an angry jackal. [14]

↬

THERE ARE NO jackals. Jackals are simply giraffes with a language problem. [30]

GIVING FROM THE HEART

THERE'S NOTHING WE human beings enjoy more, by our nature, than compassionate giving. [19]

↬

I FIND THAT my cultural conditioning leads me to focus attention on places where I am unlikely to get what I want. I developed NVC as a way to train my attention—to shine the light of consciousness—on places that have the potential to yield what I am seeking. What I want in my life is compassion, a flow between myself and others based on a mutual giving from the heart. [5]

↬

WHEN WE GIVE from the heart, we do so out of the joy that springs forth whenever we willingly enrich another person's life. This kind of giving benefits both the giver and the receiver. The receiver enjoys the gift without worrying about the consequences that accompany gifts given out of fear, guilt, shame, or desire for gain. The giver benefits from the enhanced self-esteem that results when we see our efforts contributing to someone's well-being. [5]

↬

IT'S NOT OUR objective to win. It's not our objective to get the other person to do what we want. It's our objective to create a connection that gets everybody's needs met through compassionate giving. That's different than getting the other person to do what you want. [21]

IN NONVIOLENT COMMUNICATION we try to remember: "Only give when it comes from the heart. When it's meeting your need—the strongest need that human beings have—to contribute to life." Make sure you're doing it for yourself; then the other person can benefit by it and not have to pay for it. Don't do anything out of guilt, don't do anything for rewards, don't buy love. Give from the heart. [19]

‿

THERE IS NO criticism or coercion in the NVC language. When we tell others what we want, we do so in a way that communicates to them, "Please do this only if you can do so willingly. Please never do anything for me at your expense. Never do anything for me where there is the least bit of fear, guilt, shame, resentment, or resignation behind your motives. Otherwise we'll both suffer. Please honor my request only if it comes from your heart, where it is a gift to yourself to give to me." Only when neither person feels like they're losing, giving in or giving up, do both people benefit from the action. [1]

‿

IT SEEMS TO me that if we give and receive, here's what would happen. I would do something. And you would feel this mitzvah [awareness of the blessing of an opportunity to be of service]. You would say, "Thank you for the gift." And then you respond. And then I say, "Thank you for responding that way," and you would say "Thank you for responding to my response that way," and we would spend the rest of our life celebrating. And all you did was pass me the salt. . . . And then, after about ten interchanges we would hoot, "Was I the giver or the receiver here?" Who was the giver? . . . And you see, so, any simple act we would be lost in bliss forever. [16]

‿

THE PRIMARY PURPOSE of Nonviolent Communication is to connect with other people in a way that enables giving to take place: compassionate giving. It's compassionate in that our giving comes willingly from the heart. We are giving service to others and ourselves— not out of duty or obligation, not out of fear of punishment or hope for a reward, not out of guilt or shame, but for what I consider part of our nature. It's in our nature to enjoy giving to one another. Nonviolent Communication helps us connect with one another by allowing our nature to come forward in how we give (and are given to) by others. [8]

↜

NVC IS A language that makes it possible for us to connect with one another in a way that enables us to give to each other from the heart. That means with your partner, you don't do things because of titles that imply you are *supposed to*, *should*, *ought to*, or *must*. You don't give out of guilt, shame, unconsciousness, fear, obligation, duty. It is my belief that whenever we do anything for one another out of that kind of energy, everybody loses. When we receive something given out of that kind of energy, we know we are going to have to pay for it because it was done at the other person's expense. I'm interested in a process in which we give to each other from the heart.

How do we learn to give from the heart in such a way that giving feels like receiving? When things are being done in a human way, I don't think you can tell the giver from the receiver. It's only when we interact with one another in what I call a judging, or judgmental, manner, that giving isn't much fun. [1]

↜

TO ME, GIVING of ourselves means an honest expression of what's alive in us in this moment. [6]

↜

AS A GIRAFFE-SPEAKING person, I not only want to know what I do that makes life less than wonderful for you, it's also important for me, moment by moment, to be able to connect with how you feel. Your feelings are critical for me to be aware of, if we are to play the game of giving to each other from our hearts. [23]

⌒

WHEN WE DO things that don't come out of this divine energy in each of us, this divine energy that makes compassionate giving natural, when we come out of any culturally learned pattern of doing things because we should, have to, must, out of guilt, out of shame, duty, obligation, or to get rewards, *everybody* pays for it, everybody. Nonviolent Communication wants us to be clear, to not respond unless our response is coming out of this divine energy. And you'll know it is when you are willing to do what is requested. Even if it's hard work, it will be joyful if your only motive is to make life more wonderful. [6]

⌒

WHEN BOTH PARTIES can just see what's alive in each other, nobody feels any criticism or demand. Everybody's needs can get met, through compassionate giving. [29]

⌒

COMPASSIONATE GIVING FOR me is when we do something for ourselves or others, where our sole intention is to enrich life. [31]

BLOCKS TO GIVING

THERE ARE PRIMARILY two forms of communication that make giving from the heart almost impossible for people. The first is anything that sounds to them like a criticism. . . . By *criticism*, I mean attack, judgment, blame, diagnosis, or anything that analyzes people from the head. . . . The second block to our ability to give from the heart is any hint of coercion. [1]

⤺

IT'S SO VERY precious for us to be able to do things when we choose to do them—not because somebody we love has to have it or they're going to freak out, or because they are going to keep talking at us until we do. People are very scared of spending so much of their lives having to give when it's not from the heart. So they're very reactive. [1]

⤺

I WOULD HOPE you can have some real, genuine sadness for those people who don't know how to give, because they're missing something. And what usually happens, those people we see as just the takers—the selfish—they're so scared that they're not going to get their needs met, that all of their energy goes into getting their needs met. And they provoke images that they're selfish and greedy, and . . . it's real sad that they haven't learned how to give out of mitzvah [awareness of the blessing of an opportunity to be of service]. What would be worse than not to know how to give that way? [20]

⤺

IT IS OUR nature to enjoy giving and receiving compassionately. We have, however, learned many forms of life-alienating communication that lead us to speak and behave in ways that injure others and ourselves. One form of life-alienating communication is the use of moralistic judgments that imply wrongness or badness on the part of those who don't act in harmony with our values. Another is the use of comparisons, which can block compassion both for others and for ourselves. Life-alienating communication also obscures our awareness that we are each responsible for our own thoughts, feelings, and actions. Communicating our desires in the form of demands is yet another characteristic of language that blocks compassion. [5]

～

GET OUT YOUR mental erasers and let's erase the following words from our consciousness: *right, wrong, good, bad, normal, abnormal, appropriate, inappropriate*—I don't want to go on because the list is so long. If you were educated like me, it would take us probably four or five days just to erase all the words that are in our heads that were put there through our education, that destroy this beautiful game of giving out of the heart. [22]

THE FOUR COMPONENTS OF NVC

TO ARRIVE AT a mutual desire to give from the heart, we focus the light of consciousness on four areas—referred to as the four components of the NVC model.

First, we observe what is actually happening in a situation: what are we observing others saying or doing that is either enriching or not enriching our life? The trick is to be able to articulate this observation without introducing any judgment or evaluation—to simply say what people are doing that we either like or don't like. Next, we state how we feel when we observe this action: are we hurt, scared, joyful, amused, irritated? And thirdly, we say what needs of ours are connected to the feelings we have identified. An awareness of these three components is present when we use NVC to clearly and honestly express how we are. . . .

The fourth component [is] a very specific request. . . . This fourth component addresses what we are wanting from the other person that would enrich our lives or make life more wonderful for us. [5]

～

THUS, PART OF NVC is to express these four pieces of information very clearly, whether verbally or by other means. The other part of this communication consists of receiving the same four pieces of information from others. We connect with them by first sensing what they are observing, feeling, and needing; then we discover what would enrich their lives by receiving the fourth piece—their request.

As we keep our attention focused on the areas mentioned, and help others do likewise, we establish a flow of communication, back and forth, until compassion manifests naturally: what I am observing, feeling, and needing; what I am requesting to enrich my life; what you are observing, feeling, and needing; what you are requesting to enrich your life. [5]

↜

WE WANT TO go inside of ourselves and tell people what's alive in us when they do what they do. And this involves two other kinds of literacy. First, it involves *feeling literacy* and second, *need literacy*. To say clearly what's alive in us at any given moment we have to be clear about what we feel and what we need. [8]

↜

IN NVC, NO matter what words people use to express themselves, we listen for their observations, feelings, needs, and requests. [5]

↜

AS A GIRAFFE-SPEAKING person, I am conscious that how each of us feels is a result of what our needs are and what's happening to our needs. When our needs are getting fulfilled, then we have feelings that fall under the head of pleasureful feelings. We feel happy, we feel satisfied, we feel joyful, blissful, content. [23]

↜

"
In NVC,
no matter what words
people use to express themselves,
we listen for their observations,
feelings, needs, and
requests.[5] "

WHEN WE FOCUS on clarifying what is being observed, felt, and needed rather than on diagnosing and judging, we discover the depth of our own compassion. Through its emphasis on deep listening—to ourselves as well as to others—NVC fosters respect, attentiveness, and empathy and engenders a mutual desire to give from the heart. [5]

~

LEARNING IS TOO precious to be motivated by coercive tactics. NVC is interested in learning that's motivated by reverence for life, by a desire to learn skills, to better contribute to our own well-being and the well-being of others. The particular language that contributes to helping people learn by reverence for life is called, officially, Nonviolent Communication, but for teaching purposes it is sometimes called "Giraffe Language." Its opposite—"Jackal Language"—uses words such as *ought*, *must*, and *should*. The basic vocabulary of Nonviolent Communication consists of feelings and needs.

It's important to develop a feeling and need vocabulary to assist in expressing oneself in NVC: "I feel (insert feeling) because I need (insert need)." Another basic concept in NVC is to distinguish between observation and evaluation. Observation is a clear and concise description of what is taking place. Any evaluation (judgment) of behavior is rendered in terms of feelings and needs, and by the principle of power *with*—not power *over*—people. Power-*over* leads to punishment and violence. Power-*with* leads to compassion and understanding, and to learning motivated by reverence for life rather than fear, guilt, shame, or anger. Power-*with* permits our needs to be heard as *requests* rather than demands. Demands result in defensiveness and refusal, while requests are more likely to be heard and accepted. After we've spoken our feelings and needs, we follow with a very clear request for what we want the other person to do. Requests are stated in the positive, in terms of what we do want rather than what we don't want.

In addition to expressing our needs and feelings, and expressing our needs as requests, Nonviolent Communication requires *empathic connection*, to learn how to hear any message that comes back at us as an expression of the other person's feelings and needs. In short, Nonviolent Communication is a way of keeping our consciousness tuned in moment by moment to the beauty within others and ourselves. [10]

Observations

THE FIRST COMPONENT of NVC entails the separation of observation from evaluation. When we combine observation with evaluation, others are apt to hear criticism and resist what we are saying. [5]

〜

TO TELL PEOPLE what's alive in us, we need to be able to tell them what they're doing that is supporting life in us, as well as what they're doing that isn't supporting life in us. But it's very important to learn how to say that to people without mixing in any evaluation. [8]

〜

THE INDIAN PHILOSOPHER J. Krishnamurti once remarked that observing without evaluating is the highest form of human intelligence. When I first read this statement, the thought "What nonsense!" shot through my mind before I realized that I had just made an evaluation. For most of us, it is difficult to make observations, especially of people and their behavior, that are free of judgment, criticism, or other forms of analysis. [5]

〜

ONCE YOU CAN clearly describe what you are reacting to, free of your interpretation or evaluation of it, other people are less likely to be defensive when they hear it. [34]

〜

IN NONVIOLENT COMMUNICATION, we want to be sure, whenever we want to talk to somebody about something they're doing that we're not happy with, that we clearly put this in the form of an observation. [31]

Feelings

THE FIRST COMPONENT of NVC is to observe without evaluating; the second component is to express how we are feeling. Psychoanalyst Rollo May suggests that "the mature person becomes able to differentiate feelings into as many nuances, strong and passionate experiences, or delicate and sensitive ones as in the different passages of music in a symphony." For many of us, however, our feelings are, as May would describe it, "limited like notes in a bugle call." [5]

ᕲ

WHAT MAKES US feel as we do is where we choose to place our attention. How we choose to evaluate what happened. That's what makes us feel how we do: where we place our attention and how we choose to evaluate it. [12]

ᕲ

ROLLO MAY, THE American psychologist, says that the mature human being has a feeling vocabulary, an ability to describe the life that's going on in them, that allows them to describe their life with all of the complexity of a symphony orchestra. And he said, sadly, that most of us walk around with a vocabulary in which we sound like a little tin whistle when it comes to talking about the life within us. So we haven't been taught to see the beauty in us. We've been taught to be good little boys, good little girls, good mothers, good fathers, good teachers, and that gets us disconnected from life. It gets us in our head. [10]

ᕲ

NOT ONLY AREN'T we educated to speak a language of life, a language of feelings, we have been given a cultural education that gives a very negative connotation to many of our emotions. [31]

~

NOW, IF YOU were educated as I was educated, you're going to have to do some development to build a feeling vocabulary. I went to school for twenty-one years. I can't recall ever being asked what I was feeling. The institutions I was educated in didn't seem to care about what was alive in me. It was all about getting right answers. (*Right* defined as that which the "superior" says was right.) [21]

~

THE BASIC FUNCTION of feelings is to serve our needs. The word *emotion* basically means to move us out, to mobilize us to meet our needs. So when we have a need for some nourishment, we have a feeling that we label as hunger, and that sensation stimulates us to move about to get our need for food taken care of. If we just felt comfortable each time we had a need for nourishment, we could starve, because we wouldn't be mobilized to get our need met. [9]

~

OUR FEELINGS ARE a built-in confirmation of when we have fulfilled our need to enrich life. . . . So we don't have a need for positive feelings, no, no, no! Positive feelings, pleasureful feelings, are a confirmation that our need to serve life has been met. [17]

~

IN EXPRESSING OUR feelings, it helps to use words that refer to specific emotions, rather than words that are vague or general. [5]

NEGATIVE EFFECTS CAN result when we fail to express our feelings. [4]

⟿

CERTAINLY MANY PEOPLE think that to talk about painful feelings is a negative, unpleasant experience because they associate it with guilt games, punishment, and all kinds of other stuff. They haven't seen it as part of an NVC dance and how beautiful it can be to talk about them. When I wrote the first edition of my book, I put in a list of positive feelings and a list of negative feelings. Then I noticed how people think negative feelings are negative. Since that's not what I wanted, in my next edition I put the words *positive* and *negative* in quotes, but that still didn't seem to help. Now I write, "feelings present when our needs are being met" and "feelings present when our needs are not being met" to show how valuable they both are because they are both talking about life. [1]

⟿

OUR REPERTOIRE OF words for calling people names is often larger than our vocabulary of words to clearly describe our emotional states. [5]

Feelings vs interpretations

THERE ARE DIFFERENT ways we might express our feelings, depending on what culture we grow up in, but it's important to have a vocabulary of feelings that really does just describe what's alive in us and that in no way are interpretations of other people.

   That means we don't want to use expressions like "I feel misunderstood." That's not really a feeling; it's more how we are analyzing whether the other person has understood us or not. If we think somebody has misunderstood us, we can be angry or frustrated; it could be many different things. Likewise, we don't want to use phrases like "I feel manipulated," or "I feel criticized." [8]

⟿

BE CAREFUL OF words like, *I feel misunderstood.* I feel *rejected.* I feel *criticized.* Those aren't feelings; those are sneaky jackal judgments. [21]

↜

THE WORDS I am about to say are not feelings, but are jackals in giraffe's clothing. Our language can enable us to pretend we're expressing feelings, but really what we're expressing is a judgment of the other person.

For example, *betrayed* doesn't say how you feel. It doesn't say whether you're hurt, sad, or angry. It says you have a mental image that this person is betraying you.

Here are some more words like that. I feel *misunderstood.* I feel *manipulated.* I feel *used.* I feel *criticized.* Again, I add, these are not feelings as I would define them. These are more mental images of what other people do, and more likely to cause problems than really to connect us at the heart level. [10]

Cause and responsibility for feelings

NONVIOLENT COMMUNICATION HEIGHTENS our awareness that what others say and do may be the stimulus for our feelings, but are never the cause. Our feelings result from whether our needs are being met or not. [4]

↜

WHAT OTHER PEOPLE do is a stimulus for our feelings, but it can't cause our feelings. So what causes our feelings? . . . What makes me feel as I do is my choice. [10]

↜

WE TAKE RESPONSIBILITY for our feelings. "I feel because I . . ." "You feel because you . . ." If we mix those up in the language of the day, we blur boundaries, and start to play all kinds of *un-fun* human games. [10]

FEELINGS ARE MANIFESTATIONS of what is happening to our needs. [31]

〜

FEELINGS CAN BE used in a destructive way if we try to imply that other people's behaviors are the cause of our feelings. The cause of our feelings is not other people's behavior, it's our needs. [8]

〜

FEELINGS ARE A very important part of Nonviolent Communication, but we don't . . . blame other people for our feelings. We connect our feelings to our needs. [29]

〜

WE'VE BEEN EDUCATED by people who tried to make us feel responsible for their feelings so we would feel guilty. Yes, feelings are important, but we don't want to use them in that way. We don't want to use them in a guilt-inducing manner. It's very important that when we do express our feelings, we follow that expression with a statement that makes it clear that the cause of our feelings is our needs. [8]

〜

KEEP IN MIND that other people's actions can never "make" you feel any certain way. Feelings are your warning indicators. [34]

Needs

THE THIRD COMPONENT of NVC entails the acknowledgment of the root of our feelings. NVC heightens our awareness that what others say and do may be the *stimulus*, but never the *cause*, of our feelings. We see that our feelings result from how we *choose* to receive what others say and do, as well as from our particular needs and expectations in that moment. With this third component, we are led to accept responsibility for what we do to generate our own feelings. [5]

" Feelings are a very important
part of Nonviolent Communication,
but we don't . . . blame other people
for our feelings. We connect our
feelings to our needs.[29] "

NEEDS, AS I use the term, can be thought of as resources life requires to sustain itself. For example, our physical well-being depends on our needs for air, water, rest, and food being fulfilled. Our psychological and spiritual well-being is enhanced when our needs for understanding, support, honesty, and meaning are fulfilled. [11]

⮑

SO SOMETHING AS beautiful as needs—it's the central part of what I teach, and I've never come up with words to describe it. The best I can do is *needs*. But it doesn't—for me, word-wise, it's not a beautiful enough description. What is a need to me? It's a present manifestation of divine energy within us. It's a life force. [16]

⮑

ALL WE CAN do is do the best we can with these words to get a glimmer to other people of that manifestation that's within me at this moment. I see, in the needs, this living force within me that's connected, that's interdependent with life. It makes me feel at one with a leaf. I am a leaf. . . . We are part of this beautiful universe. And look at all of the living phenomena in the universe—they have needs. Trees have needs. Bees have needs. [16]

⮑

NOW, A NEED, as I define it, is universal. All needs are universal. Anyone in the world has the same needs. So you won't see anything strange whether it's a man or a woman, regardless of religion, regardless of level of education. All human beings are created out of the same energy; they have the same needs. [25]

⮑

THERE'S NEVER A time when a person does things for no reason, or no good reason. Everything that each of us does is always for a very good reason. [14]

EVERY MOMENT EACH human being is doing the best we know at that moment to meet our needs. We never do anything that is not in the service of a need; there is no conflict on our planet at the level of needs. We all have the same needs. The problem is in strategies for meeting the needs. [34]

↝

NVC SUGGESTS BEHIND every action, however ineffective, tragic, violent, or abhorrent to us, is an attempt to meet a need. [34]

↝

WE DON'T DO anything except in service to a need. Everything we do, moment by moment in our lives, is in service of needs; it's life. [18]

↝

LIFE IS LIKE this: We have a need that needs to be met, and when it's being met, we feel a certain comfort and satisfaction. Then some needs are not getting met, some needs are getting met. . . . That, for me, is life. But the way we think about needs is that we're needy, like, "There's a needy person"—as though that's some sign of mental pathology, to be needy, you see? We think of that as what having needs means. [16]

↝

MANY PEOPLE IN fact have very negative associations with needs. They associate needs with being needy, dependent, selfish, and again I think that comes from our history of educating people to fit well into domination structures so that they are obedient and submissive to authority. See, people do not make good slaves when they're in touch with their needs. [6]

↝

THE NEED IS where the power is, because when our consciousness is need-centered, it naturally is enjoyable to give. See, that's where we are deficient in our education: in a need literacy. The part that has the power to break out of the old games of bondage is the need. That then gives us another possibility to do things on the basis of enriching life. But we don't have the literacy that has the power to do that. [22]

⤳

BUT JUST AS some jackals have a terrible time telling you what they feel, it's also very hard for jackal-speaking people to tell you what they want. Because feelings and needs or wants, in a jackal culture, are severely punished, you see. [14]

⤳

WHEN OUR FOCUS of our attention is on our needs, nature puts into us images of what to do about the need, how to meet it. But, when we don't get connected to the need, we get cut off from it by this life-alienated thinking that we have been indoctrinated with. Instead of images of how to meet the need, our head is just filled full of thoughts that leave us feeling depressed. In the book *Revolution in Psychiatry*, the anthropologist Ernest Becker says depression results from cognitively arrested alternatives. [15]

⤳

WHY ARE NEEDS important in connecting in a compassionate way? All human beings have the same needs. So when we see somebody telling us what their needs are that aren't getting met, we can identify with that. We all have the same needs. We all know how good it feels to get our needs fulfilled. So when we see a person's needs, we can better enjoy contributing to their well-being. [26]

⤳

ONE OF THE most important needs that we have is to have our needs seen for what they are . . . [for others] to see the beauty of our needs. But when, instead of getting that need met, when we get something the exact opposite of that—and we don't have giraffe ears on—it's extremely painful. Because here we're offering the most beautiful thing we have to offer: the light that is within us. [16]

꒱

I THINK THAT the need that is the most enjoyable . . . is the need to contribute to life, to enrich life. It's to be a creative force in life. [16]

꒱

WHEN WE ARE using our enormous power in the service of making life wonderful, either for ourselves or others, that's meeting one of the most basic needs that I can identify that we human beings have. This need to enrich life. [17]

꒱

NEEDS ARE NOT in conflict. The problem is our thinking. Our thinking gets in conflict. If I think I should do something, and then I think, no, I don't think that's the right thing to do. That can go on forever. But that's not getting in touch with what my needs are. I probably have two different needs there, and I'm trying to find a way to get both needs met. [19]

꒱

I BELIEVE THAT all analysis that implies wrongness is basically a tragic expression of unmet needs. If we can hear what a person needs, it's a great gift to them because it helps them to get connected to life. [11]

꒱

IT HAS BEEN my experience over and over again that from the moment people begin talking about what they need, rather than what's wrong with one another, the possibility of finding ways to meet everybody's needs is greatly increased. [5]

⤹

WHEN WE CAN connect at the need level, it's amazing how conflicts that seem unsolvable start to become solvable. We see each other's humanness at the need level. [8]

⤹

THE MORE WE are able to connect our feelings to our own needs, the easier it is for others to respond compassionately. [5]

⤹

WHEN WE EXPRESS our needs indirectly through the use of evaluations, interpretations, and images, others are likely to hear criticism. And when people hear anything that sounds like criticism, they tend to invest their energy in self-defense or counterattack. If we wish for a compassionate response from others, it is self-defeating to express our needs by interpreting or diagnosing their behavior. Instead, the more directly we can connect our feelings to our own needs, the easier it is for others to respond to us compassionately.

Unfortunately, most of us have never been taught to think in terms of needs. We are accustomed to thinking about what's wrong with other people when our needs aren't being fulfilled. [5]

⤹

WHEN WE'RE NOT able to say clearly what we need and only know how to make analyses of others that sound like criticism, wars are never far away, whether they are verbal, psychological, or physical wars. [11]

WE LEAVE THE other person out of our need. The need is in us . . . the other person isn't in us. [26]

~

OUR BODY WILL tell us when we've got the need clear. There'll be a shift in emotions. [15]

~

THE ULTIMATE AUTHORITY, I think, on whether we're really in touch with a need [is] our body. . . . Our body will tell us when we really get closer to what the need is. It's my best authority on what, at the moment, is the best language I can use: my body tells me. [25]

Needs and strategies

REGARDLESS OF OUR many differences, we all have the same needs. What differs is the strategy for fulfilling these needs. [34]

~

THE MAIN THING, to not get addicted to the strategy, is to keep the strategy and need separate. It's the need that is the energy that we want to meet. So, as soon as we get the two separate, then we can start to be conscious that there are many ways of meeting that need. But when we think that "I have a need for this particular person to love me"—now I've already made life miserable for myself, because I've gotten the need all mixed up with a particular strategy. [19]

~

AS I'M DEFINING needs, all human beings have the same needs. Regardless of our gender, educational level, religious beliefs, or nationality, we have the same needs. What differs from person to person is the strategy for fulfilling needs. I've found that it facilitates conflict resolution to keep our needs separate from the strategies that might fulfill our needs.

One guideline for separating needs from strategies is to keep in mind that needs contain no reference to specific people taking specific action. In contrast, effective strategies—or what are more commonly referred to as *wants, requests, desires,* and *solutions—do* refer to specific people taking specific actions. [11]

❧

ONE OF THE worst things that people can do to themselves is mix up needs and preferences. That takes a world which is so abundant and beautiful and shrinks it immediately into a dependence on a specific person taking a specific action. [25]

❧

THE BEST WAY to meet the needs is to make sure you don't ever get addicted to a particular strategy for meeting those needs. [19]

❧

MONEY IS NOT a need. Sex is not a need. Sexual intercourse is not a need. Sexual release, the physiological feeling, that's a need. But sexual intercourse is one way to get the need met. But money is not a need. And, boy, does our culture screw us up into thinking that it is. . . . Money is very often a helpful strategy for meeting the needs. But the problem comes when we think we need money. [19]

❧

NEEDS ARE UNIVERSAL. All human beings have the same needs. The second thing that differentiates a need from a strategy [is that] a need contains no reference to specific actions. Anytime we say "I want you to," that's not a need; that's a request or a strategy. [31]

> To hear and respect what the other person needs doesn't mean that you must do what they ask. [1]

OUR NEEDS . . . CAN be satisfied in many different ways. And whenever we trick ourselves into thinking that they can only be met by a specific person, we almost guarantee we won't get the need met. [25]

↜

TO HEAR AND respect what the other person needs doesn't mean that you must do what they ask. [1]

Needs and gender

MANY WOMEN I work with have been educated from childhood to believe that loving women have no needs. They sacrifice their needs for their family.

Likewise, men have been taught that courageous men have no needs. They're even willing to sacrifice their life for the king, for the government, for whomever. So we don't develop much of a vocabulary of needs. How can we make a clear request when we're not clear about our needs? [8]

↜

IN A WORLD where we are often harshly judged for identifying and revealing our needs, doing so can be very frightening, especially for women who are socialized to ignore their own needs while caring for others. [5]

↜

I BELIEVE THAT every message, whatever its form or content, is an expression of a need. If we accept this assumption, we can train ourselves to sense what needs might be at the root of any particular message. [11]

Requests

WHEN OUR NEEDS are not being fulfilled, we follow the expression of what we are observing, feeling, and needing with a specific request: we ask for actions that might fulfill our needs. [5]

IN NONVIOLENT COMMUNICATION, when we let a person know what they're doing that is not meeting a certain need of ours, we want to end with a clear request that is a gift to this person. It's a gift in the sense that it gives them an opportunity to do that which human beings enjoy doing: contributing to life. [21]

~

IT'S VERY IMPORTANT to know the difference between a wish and a present request. Wishes can help if you follow them at the speed of light with a clear, present request. See, the two reasons why I believe we don't get our needs met in relationships: number one, we don't express our needs, and number two, we don't express clear requests. We often think we're doing them both when we make a wish. [19]

~

WHEN WE JUST express our pain to somebody and our unmet needs, and we don't add the last thing—exactly what do you want?—then that makes it very easy for the person who's coming out of a jackal background with a lot of guilt games played on them, all the other person's supposed to do is just say, "I'm hurting," and then you're supposed to jump in and do something. So, it's a blessing to the other person if you not only say what your pain is, but what you want. [13]

~

ACTION LANGUAGE MEANS saying clearly what we do want when we make a request, using clear action verbs. It also means avoiding language that obscures our needs or sounds like an attack. [11]

~

I ALSO SUGGEST that requests be expressed in *positive action language* by stating clearly what we want done to meet our needs, rather than what we don't want. In conflict situations, telling people what we don't want creates both confusion and resistance. This applies even when we're talking to ourselves. If we just tell ourselves what we don't want to do, we're not likely to make much change in the situation. [11]

↬

WE OFTEN USE vague and abstract language to indicate how we want other people to feel or be without naming a concrete action they could take to reach that state. [5]

↬

WHEN WE EXPRESS our requests in Nonviolent Communication, they need to be very explicit. [10]

↬

NEVER GET ADDICTED to your request. [19]

Demands

WHEN MAKING A request, it is also helpful to scan our minds for the sort of thoughts that automatically transform requests into demands:

He *should* be cleaning up after himself.

She's *supposed* to do what I ask.

I *deserve* to get a raise.

I'm *justified* in having them stay later.

I have a *right* to more time off. [5]

↬

DEMANDS ARE A losing game. The more important it is that somebody do something, the more important it is that they hear what you're asking as a request, not a demand. If people hear demands, it almost guarantees they will resist. [10]

↬

IT GOES ON continuously, every day we all have needs and we all have opportunities to meet the needs of others and ourselves. This is life. It's a mitzvah [the blessing of an opportunity to be of service]. It's a memnoon [a request that blesses the one who is asked]. But I can take this beautiful thing and turn it into something ugly, by making my request a demand. Then that'll be the real test of the other person, to still hear a memnoon. [16]

෴

YOU CAN NEVER tell whether something is a request or a demand by how nicely it is asked or how clear it is. What determines the difference between a request and a demand is how we treat people when they don't do as we've asked. [6]

෴

WE DEMONSTRATE THAT we are making a request rather than a demand by how we respond when others don't comply. If we are prepared to show an empathic understanding of what prevents someone from doing as we asked, then by my definition, we have made a request, not a demand. Choosing to request rather than demand does not mean we give up when someone says no to our request. It does mean that we don't engage in persuasion until we have empathized with what's preventing the other person from saying yes. [5]

෴

WE CAN HELP others trust that we are requesting, not demanding, by indicating that we would only want them to comply if they can do so willingly. Thus we might ask, "Would you be willing to set the table?" rather than "I would like you to set the table." However, the most powerful way to communicate that we are making a genuine request is to empathize with people when they don't agree to the request. [5]

෴

WE WANT PEOPLE to act on our request only when they're connected to a kind of divine energy that exists in all of us. This divine energy is manifest in the joy we feel in giving to one another. [8]

～

USUALLY WHAT I'VE found, since I've been getting my consciousness raised, is that almost every time I hear a demand, it's because the other person is so scared to ask. They don't quite see the beauty in their own needs, they're judging themselves as being dependent, needy, whatever. And they're carrying vestiges from the past that haven't led them to see the beauty of their needs, so how sad it is for them if I continue that game by hearing it as a demand and responding out of that energy. So as soon as I hear a demand, I need to take a deep breath and try to empathize with the energy behind the other person . . . that would lead them to express it that way. [16]

～

WHEN WE BLAME others for our feelings, we are often hoping that they will feel guilty when they don't do as we have asked. The more we take a *no* as rejection or as the cause of our unhappiness, the more our requests are likely to be heard in the future as demands. [4]

～

WHEN PEOPLE HEAR demands, it looks to them as though our caring and respect and love are conditional. It looks as though we are only going to care for them as people when they do what we want. [7]

～

MY CHILDREN GAVE me some invaluable lessons about demands. Somehow I had gotten it into my head that, as a parent, my job was to make demands. I learned, however, that I could make all the demands in the world but still couldn't make my children do anything. This is a humbling lesson in power for those of us who believe that, because we're a parent, teacher, or manager, our job is to change other people and make them behave. Here were these youngsters letting me know that I couldn't make them do anything. All I could do was make them wish they had—through punishment. Then eventually they taught me that anytime I was foolish enough to make them wish they had complied by punishing them, they had ways of making me wish that I hadn't! [5]

~

OUR REQUESTS ARE received as demands when others believe they will be blamed or punished if they do not comply. When people hear a demand, they see only two options: submission or rebellion. Either way, the person requesting is perceived as coercive, and the listener's capacity to respond compassionately to the request is diminished. [5]

~

[IT IS] PROBLEMATIC . . . when people state their requests without first communicating the feelings and needs behind them. [5]

~

PEOPLE RECEIVE REQUESTS as demands if they think they will be punished or blamed if they don't do the task. When people have that idea, it takes all the joy out of doing anything. [7]

~

IF PEOPLE HEAR demands, it takes much of the joy away from doing anything. It's much more likely to provoke resistance than cooperation. [31]

~

Genuine requests

EXPRESSING GENUINE REQUESTS also requires an awareness of our objective. If our objective is only to change people and their behavior or to get our way, then NVC is not an appropriate tool. The process is designed for those of us who would like others to change and respond, but only if they choose to do so willingly and compassionately. The objective of NVC is to establish a relationship based on honesty and empathy. When others trust that our primary commitment is to the quality of the relationship, and that we expect this process to fulfill everyone's needs, then they can trust that our requests are true requests and not camouflaged demands. [5]

⤺

NEVER ASK A question or make a request when you're in a position of authority without revealing your heart first. [22]

⤺

ANSWER NO QUESTION until you first feel you are firmly connected to the person's heart behind the request. See, the question is always a request. Never respond to a request until you have first connected to the need. Takes all the joy out of doing anything that people want, if we don't see the need. [22]

TECHNIQUE VS INTENTION

I TRY NEVER to guess another person's feelings if my motive is to use Nonviolent Communication, because if I do it then it'll drive people crazy. They'll hear a mechanical technique being used on them. I want to be sure that when I guess another person's feelings and needs, it's to connect with the divine energy coming through them because I love to surf-ride. I love surf-riding. And there's no surf—even ocean surf—as fun to me as riding the divine energy that comes through us. [12]

⁀

THE MECHANICS ARE only helpful to the degree to which they support our connecting in a certain way. If we get so preoccupied with the mechanics that they become the only objective, we've lost the process.

Now, this is one of the hardest things about our training because one of the things that people say they like about our training is that it really helps them manifest in concrete ways what they've always believed. So, they like the fact that it is a way of concretely manifesting, but its very concreteness can be a disadvantage when it becomes an objective to do it "right." [2]

⁀

DURING THE INITIAL phases of learning this process, we may find ourselves applying the components of NVC mechanically without awareness of the underlying purpose. [5]

⁀

WE'RE NOT TRYING to be nice, we're trying to be real. We're trying to be honest about what goes on in us. [21]

⁀

ALTHOUGH I REFER to it as "a process of communication" or "a language of compassion," NVC is more than a process or a language. On a deeper level, it is an ongoing reminder to keep our attention focused on a place where we are more likely to get what we are seeking. [5]

⁀

WE NEED TO learn how to do what we call "speaking street giraffe." We've got to make sure that we see all human beings have the same needs. But certain cultures have different ways of talking at that level. [28]

THE IMPORTANCE OF CONNECTION

IF YOU'RE NOT connected to the life in yourself, it's going to be very hard to connect with others. [22]

∽

OUR GOAL IS to create a quality of empathic connection that allows everyone's needs to be met. [34]

∽

FOR MORE THAN forty years, I've mediated in a wide variety of conflicts between parents and children, husbands and wives, management and workers, Palestinians and Israelis, Serbians and Croatians, and warring groups in Sierra Leone, Nigeria, Burundi, Sri Lanka, and Rwanda. What I've learned from dealing with conflicts at all these levels is that it is possible to resolve conflicts peacefully and to everyone's satisfaction. The likelihood of conflicts being resolved in this fulfilling way is significantly increased if a certain quality of human connection can be established between the conflicting parties. [11]

∽

NVC HELPS US connect with each other and ourselves in a way that allows our natural compassion to flourish. [34]

∽

NOW, WHEN WE put this all together, it looks like this: We may start a dialogue with the other person by telling them what's alive in us and what we would like them to do to make life more wonderful for us. Then, no matter how they respond, we try to connect with what's alive in them and what would make life more wonderful for them. And we keep this flow of communication going until we find strategies to meet everybody's need. [8]

⌒

THERE IS ANOTHER approach besides doing nothing or using coercive tactics. It requires an awareness of the subtle but important difference between our objective being to get people to do what we want, which I'm not advocating, and instead being clear that our objective is to create the quality of connection necessary for everyone's needs to be met.

It has been my experience, whether we are communicating with children or adults, that when we see the difference between these two objectives, and we are consciously not trying to get a person to do what we want, but trying to create a quality of mutual concern, a quality of mutual respect, a quality where both parties think that their needs matter and they are conscious that their needs and the other person's well-being are interdependent—it is amazing how conflicts, which otherwise seem irresolvable, are easily resolved. [7]

⌒

NONVIOLENT COMMUNICATION IS one of the most powerful tools that I've found for connecting with people in a way that helps us get connected to the divine, where what we do toward one another comes out of divine energy. That's the place I want to get to. [6]

⌒

SO MANY TIMES I have seen that no matter what has happened, if people connect in this certain way it is inevitable that they will end up enjoying giving to one another. It is *inevitable*. For me my work is like watching the magic show. It's too beautiful for words. [6]

THE HEAVEN I gain from knowing God is this inevitability, to know it is inevitable that, no matter what the hell is going on, if we get to this level of connection with one another, if we get in touch with one another's divine energy, it's inevitable that we will enjoy giving and we'll give back to life. I've been through such ugly stuff with people that I don't get worried about it anymore. It's inevitable. If we get that quality of connection, we'll like where it gets us. [6]

⟿

I DON'T THINK you can have an authentic connection when one person is diagnosing the other. [34]

⟿

POSTPONE RESULT/SOLUTION thinking until later; it's through connection that solutions materialize—empathy before education. [34]

2

THE INTENTIONS AND CONSCIOUSNESS BEHIND NVC

NVC CONSCIOUSNESS

WHEN WE ARE living Nonviolent Communication, all we can see is the feelings and needs of the other person. [10]

༄

NVC-ERS NEVER WANT approval from other people. NVC-ers never give that power away and have other people tell them what to do. This is what we'd say in NVC:

Here's what I want. I'd like to know where you stand in relationship to that. I want to know your needs as well as mine, not because when I hear your needs I am going to give mine up or give in. I am conscious that I cannot benefit at your expense. Your needs are equally important to me as my needs. And I'm clear that doesn't ever mean having to give up my needs. [1]

༄

I'M VERY CONFIDENT that you have never done anything wrong; you never will. [15]

WE WANT TO take action out of the desire to contribute to life rather than out of fear, guilt, shame, or obligation. [34]

〜

EVERY MOMENT, EVERY living phenomenon is trying to do the most wonderful thing in the world they can. [15]

〜

IT'S IMPOSSIBLE, I believe, for somebody to see an opportunity to enrich life as other than a precious gift. [16]

〜

WHEN WE MEET that need to enrich life, we have a natural energy. It's a natural remembering, a thing we're doing every day; we start the day with a period of time to bring our consciousness to this beauty that each of us has, this power to make life wonderful. [17]

〜

WHEN WE ARE aware of the power we have to enrich life, how we can serve life, it feels good. . . . There's nothing that is better, nothing that *feels* better, nothing that's more enjoyable than using our efforts in the service of life by contributing to one another's well-being. [8]

〜

I BELIEVE THAT the most joyful and intrinsic motivation human beings have for taking any action is the desire to meet our needs and the needs of others. [34]

〜

THE FACT REMAINS that when people get connected to the needs behind the anger, frustration, and violence, they move into a different

> "We want to take action
> out of the desire to contribute to life
> rather than out of fear, guilt,
> shame, or obligation.[34]

world. They're in the world that Rumi, the thirteenth-century Sufi mystic and poet, talks about: "Out beyond ideas of wrongdoing and rightdoing there is a field: I'll meet you there." [8]

⤳

THAT WORLD THAT Rumi talks about when he says there's a place beyond rightness and wrongness . . . I'd like to spend as many moments of my life as possible in that world. [18]

⤳

ANY NEED WE have for ourselves, we have for everybody in the world. [19]

⤳

I PREDICT THAT when we have that—don't do anything that isn't play—in mind, we will see that the most fun game in the world is making life wonderful. [3]

⤳

NVC REQUIRES US to be continually conscious of the beauty within ourselves and other people. [10]

⤳

LIFE-ENRICHING HUMAN connections have three characteristics:

1. The people are empathically connected to what each is feeling and needing—they do not blame themselves or let judgments implying wrongness obscure this connection to one another.

2. The people are aware of the interdependent nature of their relationships and value the other's needs being fulfilled equally to their own needs being fulfilled—they know that their needs cannot be met at someone else's expense.

3. The people take care of themselves and one another with the sole intention of enriching their lives—they are not motivated by, nor do

they use coercion in the form of guilt, shame, duty, obligation, fear of punishment, or hope for extrinsic rewards. [4]

↬

IF TWO PEOPLE have this consciousness, all they hear ever coming from one another is a thank you or a gift. [20]

↬

NVC IS A way of keeping our consciousness tuned in moment by moment to the beauty within ourselves. [34]

↬

SO NONVIOLENT COMMUNICATION is a way of . . . not saying anything that we think might in any way tarnish people's consciousness of their own beauty. Nonviolent Communication shows us a way of being very honest, but without any criticism, without any insults, without any put-downs, without any intellectual diagnosis implying wrongness. Because the more we use words that in any way imply criticism, the more difficult it is for people to stay connected to the beauty within themselves.

And Nonviolent Communication shows us a way of staying with that beauty in ourselves and with other people, even when *they* are not using Nonviolent Communication. [10]

↬

NOTHING IS MORE enjoyable than using our efforts in the service of life. [8]

↬

ARE WE REALLY getting what we want from this moment in life? And, if not, let's do something about it! Each moment is too precious, too precious. So when our vitality is down and we're starting to become one of those nice, dead people, let's wake up. Let's do something about it. [23]

SO GIRAFFES DON'T waste any time thinking what kind of person they are. They think moment by moment about "What is the life in me at this moment?" Not "What am I?" "What is the life that's going on in me at this moment?" [23]

⤷

IF YOU ARE using Nonviolent Communication to get your way, you're not using Nonviolent Communication. [26]

⤷

WHEN WE HEAR the other person's feelings and needs, we recognize our common humanity. [34]

⤷

PEOPLE WHO SEEM like monsters are simply human beings whose language and behavior sometimes keep us from seeing their humanness. [5]

⤷

MIRACLES CAN HAPPEN when we can keep our consciousness away from analyzing and classifying one another. [34]

⤷

WHEN OUR COMMUNICATION supports compassionate giving and receiving, happiness replaces violence and grieving! [34]

⤷

ONE OF THE things that gives me seriously great pleasure is how little it takes to make human beings happy. [22]

⤷

CREATING PEACE

PEACE REQUIRES SOMETHING far more difficult than revenge or merely turning the other cheek; it requires empathizing with the fears and unmet needs that provide the impetus for people to attack each other. Being aware of these feelings and needs, people lose their desire to attack back because they can see the human ignorance leading to these attacks; instead, their goal becomes providing the empathic connection and education that will enable them to transcend their violence and engage in cooperative relationships.

When people get connected to their needs, they don't have this anger that drives them to want to punish others. We do need to make evaluations about our needs: Are they being met or not? But we do this without going up into our heads and making enemies and villains out of the people who in some way are not fulfilling our needs.

Every time we go up into our head and make a judgment of others instead of going into our heart and seeing the needs, we decrease the likelihood that other people will enjoy giving to us. [8]

I WOULD LIKE us to create peace at three levels and have each of us to know how to do it. First, within ourselves. That is to know how we can be peaceful with ourselves when we're less than perfect, for example. How we can learn from our limitations without blaming and punishing our self. If we can't do that, I'm not too optimistic how we're going to relate peacefully out in the world. Second, between people. Nonviolent Communication training shows people how to create peace within themselves and at the same time how to create connections with other people that allows compassionate giving to take place naturally. And third, in our social systems. To look out at the structures that we've created, the governmental structures and other structures, and to look at whether they support peaceful connections between us and if not, to transform those structures. [34]

I BELIEVE, AS did Teilhard de Chardin, that a peaceful world is not only possible, it's inevitable. I think we're evolving in that direction. Of course, he was very patient because he was a paleontologist; he thought in terms of tens of thousands of years. And he wasn't naïve about all the violence that's going on now, but he saw the violence as just an evolutionary snag. He sees our evolution, and I do, too, but I'm not as patient as he is. I can't wait thousands of years for it, so I'm interested in how we can speed it up. But I think it's inevitable and, unless we destroy the planet in the meantime, I think we're moving in that direction.

I, along with my associates at the Center for Nonviolent Communication, will continue to provide this education for people so they can create a world within themselves that will support and sustain an outer world of peace. We do this because we want people to know how to create peace in their relationships—and also know the power they have to create structures that support compassionate interactions, compassionate exchanges of resources, and compassionate justice. [8]

BEING SELF-FULL

GIRAFFE REQUIRES A consciousness of self-full-ness. In jackal land we only know *selfish, selfless*. We're now bringing in a whole different concept of *self-full-ness*. So anything that persons do for another person that isn't done purely out of self-full-ness, we pay for in this way: it is taking them away from the divine game we're talking about. [16]

‿ᔱ

GIRAFFES NEVER MEET anybody's needs but their own. They are self-full. Not to be confused with selfish. Not to be confused with selfless. Self-full. [22]

IF I'VE BEEN educated to be selfless, I'm not giving other people the opportunity to nurture. To meet their need for giving. If I'm the only giver, I'm hogging the good stuff. [16]

❧

WHAT WE CALL selfishness is, I would say, tragic self-full-ness. [18]

❧

THE PEOPLE THAT I'm calling self-full realize that we don't do anything for others. We do things only for ourselves and what is the most fun game in town? Contributing to people's well-being. So, we do that to meet our need for meaning, for purpose in life, joy. The joy comes in enriching life for others, you see; we're doing that for ourselves. That's the most fun game in town. [18]

❧

SELFISHNESS IS JUST limited self-full-ness. You get some needs met but at the cost of others. If I put in all of this energy to get this one need met . . . I'm ruining my chance of getting other very important needs met. So I'm really not taking very good care of myself. [18]

❧

WE'VE BEEN SO deeply ingrained with, and so exposed to tactics motivated to get us to do what's good for us and society through those tactics, that it's pretty hard to get pure giving going between human beings. So that's why I like to check myself, to make sure I never do anything for others, never, only for self-full reasons. Only when it's play. [16]

❧

SEEING NEEDS AS A GIFT

IF OUR PARENTS were in so much pain because their needs weren't getting met, it's very likely that every message that we got—or many of the messages we got—[with regard] to our needs was a message of pain, instead of somebody receiving a gift. And . . . we didn't have giraffe ears, so we started to conclude that what's alive in us is something ugly. [16]

⸺

THE MOST IMPORTANT part of expressing our needs is really not even the language we use, it's the consciousness we have about what our needs are. See, the culture we've been educated in educates us to think that to have needs is to be needy, dependent, weak, selfish. So, then, when we have carried that consciousness with us, when we do get our courage up to express our needs and requests, we do it with what I call a "kick-me" energy. [19]

⸺

MOST OF US need to do a lot of work to come to see our needs as a gift, which I think they are. It's what's alive in us. And to add a request to the other person, gives them another gift—an opportunity to do what human beings like more than anything else, to enrich life. So if we have that energy, that consciousness, the mechanics of the words are secondary. It's that consciousness about our needs which is the hardest to develop . . . to see our needs as a gift. [19]

⸺

PEOPLE DON'T MAKE good slaves when they see their needs as a gift. [19]

⸺

IF THE OTHER person accurately hears your need, they'll receive a gift. That's helped me immensely. So as soon as I see in the other person's eyes, you know, I know they didn't receive the need. The damn jackal postal delivery service. I sent out a beautiful gift, they delivered something ugly. But I don't want to assume that it's my need that can ever stimulate those looks or "Do it yourself" or "What do you think I am, a slave?" [19]

〜

AND I'VE TRIED to look inside myself, to try to find out, why do I still have so much trouble seeing my needs as beautiful? And it came to me one day: because of how many people have given to me out of energy other than memnoon [a request that blesses the one who is asked]. Am I afraid that people will say no? No, I don't have any fear of no; hardly ever have people said no to me. I'm much more afraid of a *yes*—that people have given with that other stuff mixed in, so then it leads me to associate my need with a burden. [20]

FINDING OUR NATURAL COMPASSION

NVC HELPS US connect with each other and ourselves in a way that allows our natural compassion to flourish. It guides us to reframe the way we express ourselves and listen to others by focusing our consciousness on four areas: what we are observing, feeling, and needing, and what we are requesting to enrich our lives. NVC fosters deep listening, respect, and empathy and engenders a mutual desire to give from the heart. [5]

〜

WHEN WE ARE internally violent toward ourselves, it is difficult to be genuinely compassionate toward others. [5]

〜

WHAT I WANT in my life is compassion, a flow between myself and others based on a mutual giving from the heart. [5]

CREATING LIFE-ENRICHING SYSTEMS

IF YOU WANT to serve life, you want to create life-enriching systems.[3]

∽

LIFE-ENRICHING IS THE key concept in my paradigm: every action comes out of an image of seeing how human needs would be met by the action. That's the vision that mobilizes everything. A life-enriching organization is one in which all work in the organization, everything that every worker does, comes out of seeing how it's going to support life in the form of meeting needs—needs of the physical planet, trees, lakes, or human beings or animals—and it's clear how life will be served through meeting of needs. And that's the vision that inspires the actions, purely. In a life-enriching structure, nobody works for money. Money plays the same role as food for a mother who is breastfeeding her infant. She doesn't receive food as payment. The food is nurturance so she has the energy to serve life. It all boils down to human needs, which is why Nonviolent Communication is so rooted in the consciousness of needs. Everything we do is in the service of needs and the pleasure that is felt when needs are fulfilled, especially spiritual needs. Those are the most fun needs to fulfill.

To me, the bees and the flowers are part of a life-enriching organization. Look at how they both meet each other's needs. They don't do it through any guilt, duty, or obligation, but naturally, in a natural system. The bee gets its nectar from the flower and it pollinates the flower.[3]

∽

IT IS HARD to separate meeting human needs from the needs of the environment: They are one and the same. Meeting the needs of all the phenomena on the planet. Seeing the oneness of it all. Seeing the beauty in that whole scheme, that whole interdependent scheme of life. Life-enriching structures—the kind of structures that I would like to see us creating and participating in—are structures whose vision is to serve

> **What I want in my life is compassion, a flow between myself and others based on a mutual giving from the heart.** [5]

life. And how do we know if an organization—whether it's a family, or work team, or government—is a life-serving organization? We find out by asking: Is its mission to meet the needs and enrich the lives of people within—and affected by—the organization? [3]

⮑

LIFE-ENRICHING ORGANIZATIONS are characterized by fairness and equity in how resources and privileges are distributed. People in positions of leadership *serve* their constituencies rather than desiring to control them. The nature of laws, rules, and regulations are consensually defined, understood, and willingly followed. [4]

⮑

LIFE-ENRICHING ORGANIZATIONS, whether families, schools, businesses, or governments, value the well-being of each person in the community or organization and support life-enriching connections between the members of the group. [4]

⮑

IN A LIFE-ENRICHING organization, we get what we want but never at someone else's expense—getting what we want at someone else's expense cannot fulfill all our needs. Our goal in a life-enriching organization is far more beautiful—to express our needs without blaming others and to listen respectfully to others' needs, without anyone giving up or giving in—and thus create a quality of connection through which everyone's needs can be met. [4]

THE SPIRITUALITY OF NVC

NVC IS A combination of thinking and language, as well as a means of using power designed to serve a specific intention. This intention is to create the quality of connection with other people and oneself that allows compassionate giving to take place. In this sense it is a spiritual practice: All actions are taken for the sole purpose of willingly contributing to the well-being of others and ourselves. [8]

~

THE SPIRITUALITY EMBODIED in NVC exists not so much to help people connect with the divine as to come from the divine energy we're created out of, our natural life-serving energy. It's a living process to keep us connected to the life within our self and the life that's going on in other people. [8]

~

THE SPIRITUALITY WE embrace is to make people conscious moment by moment that our purpose in life comes from compassionate giving, compassionate service. There's nothing more wonderful than exercising our power in the service of life. That's a manifestation of the divine energy within us, and that is our greatest joy: to use our efforts in the service of life. [8]

~

I THINK IT is important that people see that spirituality is at the base of Nonviolent Communication, and that they learn the mechanics of the NVC process with that in mind. It's really a spiritual practice that I am trying to show as a way of life. Even though we don't make a point of mentioning this, people get seduced by the practice. Even if they practice NVC as a mechanical technique, they start to experience things between themselves and other people they weren't able to experience before. So eventually they come to the spirituality of the process. They begin to see that it's more than a communication process and realize it's really an attempt to manifest our spirituality. [6]

I NEED A way to think of God that works for me—other words or ways to look at this beauty, this powerful energy—and so my name for God is "beloved divine energy." For a while it was just "divine energy" but then I was reading some of the Eastern religions, and Eastern poets, and I loved how they had this personal, loving connection with this energy. And I found that it added to my life to call it "beloved divine energy." To me this beloved divine energy is life, connection to life. [6]

I KNOW BELOVED divine energy by connecting with human beings in a certain way. I not only see divine energy, I taste divine energy, I feel divine energy, and I am divine energy. I'm connected with beloved divine energy when I connect with human beings in this way. Then God is very alive for me. [6]

NONVIOLENT COMMUNICATION HELPS me stay connected with that beautiful divine energy within myself and to connect with it in others. And certainly when I connect that divine energy within myself with the divine energy in others, what happens is the closest thing to knowing what it is to be connected to God. [6]

WE ARE THIS divine energy. It's not something we have to attain. We just have to realize it, to be present to it. [34]

BEFORE WE TACKLE the gangs [groups that behave in ways we don't like, whether street gangs, corporations, or governments] . . . we have to make sure that we have liberated ourselves from how we have been educated and make sure we are coming from a spirituality of our own choosing. [34]

GET VERY CLEAR about the kind of world we would like and then start living that way. [34]

❧

OUR SURVIVAL AS a species depends on our ability to recognize that our well-being and the well-being of others are in fact one and the same. [34]

❧

THE KIND OF spirituality I value is one in which you get great joy out of contributing to life, not just sitting and meditating, although meditation is certainly valuable. But from the meditation, from the resulting consciousness, I would like to see people in action, creating the world that they want to live in. [6]

❧

UNLESS WE AS social change agents come from a certain spirituality, we're likely to create more harm than good. What I mean by spirituality is that, moment by moment, we're staying connected to our own life and to the lives of others. And we can discover our spirituality by asking: What is the good life? What are we about? This quality of consciousness will help lead us to a life-enriching spirituality that helps us connect with ourselves and others at the heart level. [3]

UNDERSTANDING CHOICE

WHEN YOU'RE REALLY free, you're aware that you can do whatever you choose to do every moment of your life. Nobody can make you do anything. [3]

❧

USE THE WORDS *I feel because I* to remind us that what we feel isn't because of what the other person did, but because of a choice I've made. [34]

" How I choose to look at any
situation will greatly affect whether
I have the power to change it or
make matters worse. [34] "

WHEN WE SPEAK a language that denies choice, we forfeit the life in ourselves for a robot-like mentality that disconnects us from our own core. [5]

SEE, WITH GIRAFFES, it's not a matter of knowing what's right and going with it. To be a giraffe requires choosing what you want. Choosing. It's based more on intuition. It's not thinking. It's more being really in touch with your unmet needs, and then choosing what you want to do about it. [23]

PEOPLE ARE SCARED of having their autonomy taken away. It's so precious to us, to just do things when we choose to do them. . . . And all over the world, you know what? People give it away. They give it away to authorities, have authority tell them what's right. So that's a funny thing about human beings. They want this autonomy so much, but they're giving it away all the time. [23]

THAT'S A VERY important need, to make our own choices. From the time we see we're a different person, at age two, that's a very strong need. [26]

NO HUMAN BEING has ever done anything that they didn't choose to do. Most people have been programmed to believe they have no choice, because that helps to educate you to be a nice dead person. [27]

HOW I CHOOSE to look at any situation will greatly affect whether I have the power to change it or make matters worse. [34]

WE DON'T DO anything that isn't in the service of our needs. We don't say anything or do anything . . . that we don't choose to do. I'm not saying we like it, [that] we like doing it. I'm saying we don't do anything we don't choose to do. [27]

⌒

THE PROCESS IS wonderful. That every living phenomenon in every moment is searching for a way of making life wonderful. I'm not saying the choices we make are wonderful. Very often we pick strategies that don't work. Not only do they not make life wonderful, they make life miserable. But every moment, we need to see that our chooser's intent is to make life wonderful. It's doing the best it knows to serve life at every moment. And that's wonderful. [15]

PART II

BARRIERS TO EMBODYING NVC

> We're not that complicated . . .
> We all have the same needs.[24]

3

HOW CULTURAL CONDITIONING
GETS IN THE WAY

WE'VE ALL LEARNED things that limit us as human beings, whether from well-intentioned parents, teachers, clergy, or others. Passed down through generations, even centuries, much of this destructive cultural learning is so ingrained in our lives that we are no longer conscious of it. In one of his routines, comedian Buddy Hackett, raised on his mother's rich cooking, claimed that he never realized it was possible to leave the table without feeling heartburn until he was in the army. In the same way, pain engendered by damaging cultural conditioning is such an integral part of our lives that we can no longer distinguish its presence. It takes tremendous energy and awareness to recognize this destructive learning and to transform it into thoughts and behaviors that are of value and of service to life. [5]

꠸

WE'RE NOT THAT complicated, we human beings. We all have the same needs. It's just that we have been educated . . . to justify pretty brutal ways of getting our needs met. [24]

"In our culture, most of us have been
trained to ignore our own wants
and to discount our needs. [34]

WHEN YOU HAVE structures that are not doing too well at really serving people, but that are based on some thinking that's been going on for about eight thousand years, which causes a lot of violence on our planet . . . you're going to have a lot of people very depressed. But not because they have a disease—because of the way we educate people to fit into the structures we've created. You're going to have a lot of violence, directed both outward and inward. [19]

༗

THE GOVERNMENTAL STRUCTURES we've been programmed to live within require making people nice, dead people who do what the superiors tell them is right to do. Well, so that's why we use guilt tactics, shame tactics, punishment, rewards: to maintain those structures which create the violence on our planet. [21]

༗

PEOPLE HAVE BEEN trained to criticize, insult, and otherwise communicate in ways that create distance among people. [34]

༗

WE'VE BEEN BROUGHT up, educated under domination systems, the purpose of which is to teach you to be docile and subservient to authority. So we've learned a language that doesn't help us to say how we are and what would make life more wonderful. [22]

༗

IN OUR CULTURE, most of us have been trained to ignore our own wants and to discount our needs. [34]

༗

WHEN WE'RE FULLY in touch with our needs, nature puts into our heads images of how to meet those needs. But education in domination cultures blocks this natural process and turns our consciousness of the need into a misrecognition of a need. [25]

⬳

WE'VE BEEN PROGRAMMED for eight thousand years in this language of violence, in a language that teaches us to judge one another: right, wrong, good, bad, normal, abnormal, freedom fighter, terrorist. To turn people into objects, into things that justify punishment, reward. [29]

⬳

SCHOOLING TEACHES US to dehumanize human beings by thinking of what they are, rather than what they need. [34]

⬳

WHEN PEOPLE HEAR needs, it provokes compassion. When people hear diagnoses, it provokes defensiveness and attack. [34]

⬳

FOUR Ds OF Disconnection: (1) Diagnosis (judgment, analysis, criticism, comparison); (2) Denial of Responsibility; (3) Demand; (4) *Deserve*-oriented language. [34]

4

THE TRAGEDY OF JUDGMENT

RIGHT AND WRONG

THERE ARE WHOLE cultures that do not have the word *wrong* in their consciousness. They have far less violence than we do. [12]

↬

AS A GIRAFFE, you're conscious that you never do anything wrong. . . . It's probably the hardest thing about giraffe—to be aware that we never do anything wrong. We're doing the best we can each moment. [23]

↬

WE WANT TO be honest in Nonviolent Communication, but we want to be honest without using words that imply wrongness, criticism, insult, judgment, or psychological diagnosis. [8]

↬

MOST OF US don't know what we want. It's only after we get something and it messes up our life that we know it wasn't what we wanted. I'll say I want an ice cream cone, get one, eat it, then feel terrible and realize that wasn't what I wanted. To an NVC-er, it's not a matter of knowing what is right or wrong. To use the language of life requires courage and choosing what you want based more on intuition than thinking. It's being in touch with your unmet needs and choosing what you want to do about them. [1]

～

THE ULTIMATE GOAL is to spend as many of my moments in life as I can in that world that the poet Rumi talks about, a place beyond rightness and wrongness. [2]

～

THE SUFI POET Rumi once wrote, "Out beyond ideas of wrongdoing and rightdoing, there is a field. I'll meet you there." Life-alienating communication, however, traps us in a world of ideas about rightness and wrongness—a world of judgments. It is a language rich with words that classify and dichotomize people and their actions. When we speak this language, we judge others and their behavior while preoccupying ourselves with who's good, bad, normal, abnormal, responsible, irresponsible, smart, ignorant, etc. [5]

～

LONG BEFORE I reached adulthood, I learned to communicate in an impersonal way that did not require me to reveal what was going on inside myself. When I encountered people or behaviors I either didn't like or didn't understand, I would react in terms of their wrongness. If my teachers assigned a task I didn't want to do, they were "mean" or "unreasonable." If someone pulled out in front of me in traffic, my reaction would be, "You idiot!" When we speak this language, we think and communicate in terms of what's wrong with others for behaving in certain ways or, occasionally, what's wrong with ourselves for not understanding or responding as we would like. Our attention is focused on classifying, analyzing, and determining levels of wrongness rather than on what we and others need and are not getting. Thus if my partner wants more affection than I'm giving her, she is "needy and dependent." But if I want more affection than she is giving me, then she is "aloof and insensitive." If my colleague is more concerned about details than I am, he is "picky and compulsive." On the other hand, if I am more concerned about details than he is, he is "sloppy and disorganized."

It is my belief that all such analyses of other human beings are tragic expressions of our own values and needs. They are tragic because when we express our values and needs in this form, we increase defensiveness and resistance among the very people whose behaviors are of concern to us. Or, if people do agree to act in harmony with our values, they will likely do so out of fear, guilt, or shame because they concur with our analysis of their wrongness. [5]

JUDGMENT

WHEN WE JUDGE others we contribute to violence. [34]

⌐

NONVIOLENT COMMUNICATION SHOWS us a way of being very honest, but without any criticism, without any insults, without any put-downs, without any intellectual diagnosis implying wrongness. [10]

⌐

ANOTHER FORM OF judgment is the use of comparisons. [5]

⌐

THE MORE UGLY the judgment, the more beautiful the need behind it. [16]

INTERPRETATIONS, CRITICISMS, DIAGNOSES, and judgments of others are actually alienated expressions of our unmet needs. [4]

〜

BE CONSCIOUS THAT all judgments like *should* and *unfair* are tragic expressions of needs. Translate *should* and *unfair* into your needs. [26]

〜

JUDGMENTS OF OTHERS contribute to self-fulfilling prophecies. [34]

〜

WHETHER I PRAISE or criticize someone's action, I imply that I am their judge, that I'm engaged in rating them or what they have done. [34]

〜

NEVER QUESTION THE beauty of what you are saying because someone reacts with pain, judgment, criticism. It just means they have not heard you. [34]

〜

I BELIEVE THAT anytime we influence people with criticism, blame, insults—even if they do what we request—it will be very costly to us. [31]

〜

THE MORE PEOPLE hear blame and judgment, the more defensive and aggressive they become and the less they will care about our needs in the future. [5]

〜

THE THOUGHTS THAT are the hardest for me to deal with are the ones that I am already thinking myself. So, then I get very easily caught up in that world of judgment. It makes it harder to come back to life. [27]

> " The more people hear blame
> and judgment, the more defensive
> and aggressive they become and the
> less they will care about our
> needs in the future. [5] "

AS SOON AS we judge someone as "sexist" or "racist," even if we don't say the judgment out loud, but just carry it in our head, we have almost no power to get what we need. [1]

❧

THE MORE PEOPLE go around with *should*s in their heads, and fearful of doing things wrong, wondering what other people might think of them—how can you possibly celebrate life? For example, if you think there is such a thing as being intelligent, how can you enjoy life? You're going to spend so much of your time wondering about what you say, whether what you think and do is dumb, you can't enjoy life. [17]

❧

THE MORE DIRECTLY we can connect our feelings to our needs, the easier it is for others to respond compassionately. On the other hand, when our needs are expressed through interpretations and judgments, people are likely to hear criticism. [4]

❧

IF YOU WANT to make life miserable for yourself, when somebody behaves in a way you don't like, think of what is wrong with the person for doing what they did. Now, if you want to make life even more miserable for yourself, tell the person what you think is wrong with them. . . . All criticism, all blame, any diagnosis of the other person that implies wrongness on their part, is a losing game. [21]

❧

WHEN WE HAVE a judgment in our head that this person is rude, we pay for it. If we hear somebody else telling us we're rude, we pay for it. We're living in a world of rudeness. Not a fun world. Not a natural world. In the natural world needs are being met or not being met all the time, whether it's the planet, human beings, dogs, cats. It's a world of love. It's a different world. [27]

⤳

LIFE-SERVING JUDGMENTS ARE based on human needs. Whether actions are serving life or not. Whether they're meeting human needs. We need to make these kinds of judgments. We can't survive very long without measuring everything we do in terms of "Is it meeting our needs?" But that's not to be mixed up with the judgments that are made in retributive justice. Judgments that determine whether people deserve reward or punishment. Let's not get life-serving judgments mixed up with those. [19]

⤳

IT IS IMPORTANT here not to confuse *value judgments* and *moralistic judgments*. All of us make *value judgments* as to the qualities we value in life; for example, we might value honesty, freedom, or peace. Value judgments reflect our beliefs of how life can best be served. We make *moralistic judgments* of people and behaviors that fail to support our value judgments; for example, "Violence is bad. People who kill others are evil." Had we been raised speaking a language that facilitated the expression of compassion, we would have learned to articulate our needs and values directly, rather than to insinuate wrongness when they have not been met. [5]

⤳

OVER THE YEARS, I have come to see that these kinds of judgments of others that make us angry are not only alienated expressions of our needs, but at times they look to me like they are suicidal, tragic expressions of our needs. Instead of going to our heart to get connected to what we need and are not getting, we direct our attention to judging what is wrong with other people for not meeting our needs. When we do this, a couple of things are likely to happen.

First, our needs are not likely to get met, because when we verbally judge other people as wrong in some way, these judgments usually create more defensiveness than learning or connection. At the very least, they don't create much cooperation. Even if people do things we would like them to do after we have judged them as wrong or lazy or irresponsible, they will take these actions with an energy that we will pay for. We will pay for it because when we are angry as a result of judging people— and we express these judgments to them either verbally or through our nonverbal behavior—they pick up that we are judging them as wrong in some way. Even if people then do what we would like them to do, they are likely to be motivated more out of fear of being punished, fear of being judged, out of their guilt or shame, than out of compassion in relation to our needs.

When we are using NVC, we remain conscious at all times that it's as important why people do what we would like them to do, as it is that they do it. So we are conscious that we only want people to do things willingly, and not do things because they think they're going to be punished, blamed, "guilted," or shamed if they don't. [9]

っ

WITH A GREATER vocabulary of needs, we are able to more easily get in touch with the needs behind the judgments that are making us angry. For it's when we can clearly express our needs that others have a much greater likelihood of responding compassionately to whatever it is we would like. [9]

っ

THE MORE PEOPLE are trained to think in terms of moralistic judgments that imply wrongness and badness, the more they are being trained to look outside themselves—to outside authorities—for the definition of what constitutes right, wrong, good, and bad. When we are in contact with our feelings and needs, we humans no longer make good slaves and underlings. [5]

Criticism

CRITICISM IS NEVER honest. [26]

~

THE MORE WE use words that in any way imply criticism, the more difficult it is for people to stay connected to the beauty within themselves. [34]

~

WHEN PEOPLE DO not feel criticized, they don't have to put all of their energy into defense. They can start to look for some other option. [10]

~

THERE IS NO such thing as criticism. What we hear as criticism is a painful expression of *please*. [22]

~

THERE IS NO criticism. If you are a giraffe, there is no criticism; it does not exist. You are aware that what used to look like criticism when you wore jackal ears, you now see as a suicidal, tragic expression of an unmet need. That's all you hear: a need that's being expressed in a way that's going to be hard to get met by anyone that doesn't have giraffe ears on. [22]

~

IN FACT, WHEN we have giraffe ears on, we never fear what somebody thinks about us. You'll live longer—you'll enjoy human beings more—if you never hear what they think about you. No, we don't hear what they think. [21]

~

THERE'S NOT ONLY no criticism in the language of giraffe, but no coercion. [23]

> "Hearing the truth will set us free
> from all kinds of self-induced
> damage that comes from ever
> hearing criticism.[27]

WE PAY DEARLY for every criticism people receive from us. We pay dearly for every guilt trip we lay on other people. If we saw how much we pay, we would never use criticism or guilt—we'd never do it. [21]

෧

I THINK WHEN a person is saying something that we used to hear as an attack, criticism, diagnosis, psychological analysis, or implies wrongness, the truth, I believe, is that they have a need that isn't getting met and they're in pain. And hearing the truth will set us free from all kinds of self-induced damage that comes from ever hearing criticism. [27]

෧

IF I HAVE giraffe ears on, I can't hear criticism or praise. I can only hear the truth. [26]

Positive Judgments

COMPLIMENTS AND PRAISE, for their part, are tragic expressions of fulfilled needs. [34]

෧

THE WORST DANGER of all about compliments or praise—the other person might believe it. And it is just as dehumanizing to believe you're a nice person as to believe you're a rat. They both reduce you to a thing, so any compliment is reducing the other person to a thing. . . . They're still part of the jackal game. Positive judgments are still one person passing judgment on another. [17]

෧

PRAISE AND COMPLIMENTS are basically the same game as criticism and blame. That's a language that got started many centuries ago, when we decided to have domination structures governing us. Where some people are called superiors and others are called inferiors.

And in those societies that think that way, the superiors . . . have the right to use punishment and reward to maintain control. [21]

～

IN NONVIOLENT COMMUNICATION, we suggest not giving compliments or praise. In my view, telling somebody they did a good job, that they're a kind or competent person . . . that's still using moralistic judgments. That's still creating a world different from the world Rumi is talking about when he says there's a place beyond rightdoing and wrongdoing. When we're using judgmental words for praise and compliments, it's the same *form* of language as telling somebody they're unkind, stupid, or selfish.

We suggest that positive judgments are equally as dehumanizing to people as negative judgments. We also suggest how destructive it is to give positive feedback as a reward. Don't dehumanize people by complimenting them or praising them. [8]

5

THE POWER OF LANGUAGE

LANGUAGE AND VIOLENCE

OUR LANGUAGE WAS a language designed to teach us to be obedient to authority. So that's a pretty big jump, from that language to one that . . . focuses attention on the beauty of life each moment. [16]

↶

MOST OF US grew up speaking a language that encourages us to label, compare, demand, and pronounce judgments rather than to be aware of what we are feeling and needing. [5]

↶

OFTEN, THE USE of vague and abstract language can mask oppressive interpersonal games. [5]

↶

IT'S TYPICAL OF human beings that when we need to be understood the most, we communicate in a way that makes it the hardest for other people to do. [30]

WHILE WE MAY not consider the way we talk to be "violent," our words often lead to hurt and pain, whether for others or for ourselves. [34]

⬿

WHY **QUESTIONS ARE** one of the most violent forms of communication we've ever developed. . . . *Why* questions are often asked by teachers and parents and managers and bosses on a fault-finding mission: if you give the wrong answer to the *why* question, you get punished. You see, they're looking for evidence to know if you deserve to suffer or not for what you've done. That's the jackal justice system; it's called retributive justice. [12]

⬿

IN NVC, ALL names [in the sense of *name-calling*] are tragic expressions of unmet needs. An NVC-er asks himself, when the names are coming at him, "What is this person wanting that they're not getting?" Tragically, they don't know any other way of saying the need except to call the name. [1]

⬿

THE FIRST THING in the schools of the kind we're trying to support the creation of in our network—we sometimes call them giraffe schools, life-serving schools... [is that] all the people—parents, teachers, students—all speak the language of Nonviolent Communication. They're all trained in it. Note that we have an alarm at the door, a detector that teachers have to go through on the way in. No teacher is allowed in the school if they have these words in their consciousness: *right, wrong, correct, incorrect, slow learner, fast learner, emotionally disturbed, normal.* No teacher is allowed in the school who has those violent words in their head. [18]

⬿

SO, WE'VE BEEN living under a destructive mythology for a long time and that destructive mythology requires a certain language. It requires a language that dehumanizes people, turns them into objects. So we have learned to think in terms of moralistic judgments of one another. We have words in our consciousness like *right, wrong, good, bad, selfish, unselfish, terrorists, freedom fighters.* And connected to these is the concept of justice based on *deserve,* that if you do one of these bad things you deserve to be punished. If you do the good things then you deserve to be rewarded. Unfortunately, for about eight thousand years we have been subjected to that consciousness. I think that's the core of violence on our planet: faulty education. The process of Nonviolent Communication is an integration of thought, language, and communication that I think brings us closer to our nature. It helps us to connect with one another so that we come back to what is really the fun way to live, which is contributing to one another's well-being. [6]

THE DANGER OF WORDS

NEVER PUT YOURSELF in any box with the verb *to be.* That's too limiting to you as a human being to ever think of what you are. Like, somebody has asked me, "Well, are you a man or a woman?" I'll say, "Some of the above, none of the above, all of the above and more, of course." "Are you stupid, or intelligent?" "Some of the above, none of the above, all of the above and more, of course." [12]

UNTIL YOU UNDERSTAND that the map is not the territory, you're not aware of the danger of words. Words are never what they describe. It's so obvious, on the one hand, but we actually don't realize the meaning we ascribe to the phenomenon by the words we put on it. [16]

WE'VE BEEN TAUGHT, I believe, a suicidal language—that when we need empathy the most, we are communicating in a way that makes it the hardest for people to give it to us. And if that isn't a suicidal language, what is? When we need safety the most, we think that some people are terrorists. When we need support the most, we say to somebody they're lazy. When we need love and connection the most, we say "You're insensitive to my needs." What a tragic, suicidal language we've been taught. [12]

⸙

NAMES [IN THE sense of *name-calling*] are simply tragic expressions of unmet needs. NVC-ers know that there is no such thing as *normal, abnormal, right, wrong, good,* or *bad.* They know that all of those are a product of language that trained people to live under a king. If you want to train people to be docile to a higher authority, to fit into hierarchical structures in a subservient way, it is very important to get people up in their head and to get them thinking what is "right," what is "normal," what is "appropriate," and to give that power to an authority at the top who defines what those are. [1]

⸙

AND THEN ALONG with moralistic judgments, you need a language that obscures choice. Words that imply we have no choice except to do what authority says is right. Words like *have to, should, ought to, must, can't, supposed to.* And then you need this very important concept if you want to maintain a domination structure such as our judicial system and economic systems, the concept of deserve, or worth. It's very important in maintaining domination structures to get people to believe that certain actions deserve reward, certain actions deserve punishment. [3]

⸙

THERE'S TWO KINDS of pain: that pain that comes from just staying with life and being with mourning a loss, and then there's this other kind of pain that comes from *should* kind of thinking. *This shouldn't have happened to me, it isn't fair . . .* and that's the kind of pain I'm saying we don't have to deal with. [13]

LABELING

I'VE HEARD A lot of people who get a lot out of saying, "I'm codependent, I'm alcoholic," and they feel a lot better because that's better than telling themselves, "I'm a total shit." So now they have something that makes them feel less bad about themselves. But I'm concerned about that because it leads to labeling and classifying. It's static language, you see? And I'm worried about static language. So I would really like the strengths of Alcoholics Anonymous and the codependency program to be maintained—and that is empathy for what you're doing. See, people get a lot of empathy by people understanding why they're doing what they're doing. I just wish we could take the strength of that out without labeling people. [14]

↝

AS SOON AS I'm thinking what this person *is*, it detracts from my ability to purely connect with what they're feeling and needing. That requires that I not bring any labels, any diagnosis, to this moment. Every moment must be like a newborn infant that has never been before or ever will be again. And so any labels that I have stuck in my head about what this person *is*, colors my ability to hear. And actually leads to self-fulfilling prophecies. [14]

↝

I THINK EVEN if I don't say the label out loud—if I think this person is behaving in a passive-aggressive way, for example, I don't have to say "I think you are behaving in a passive-aggressive way." When we think that way about people, we have jackal eyes. When we're up in our head analyzing people, we have quite a different demeanor than when we are fully trying to connect with what that person is saying. [14]

⤳

THESE LABELS OF . . . *right/wrong, good/bad, normal/abnormal* . . . any kind of label that's static about a human being, is missing the human being. Because human beings change from moment to moment. Therefore, if we want to understand human beings, we need a process language, not a static language. [14]

⤳

UNFORTUNATELY, THE LANGUAGE we have learned has taught us to judge our own actions and the actions of others in terms of moralistic categories such as *right/wrong, correct/incorrect, good/bad, normal/ abnormal, appropriate/inappropriate.*

We have been further educated to believe that persons in positions of authority know which of these judgments best fits any situation. If we find ourselves wearing the label *teacher* or *principal*, we think we should know what is best for all those we supervise, and we are quick to label those who do not comply with our decisions as *uncooperative, disruptive,* or even *emotionally disturbed.* At the same time, we are calling ourselves *ineffective* if our efforts fail. Our having been educated to use language in this way contributes to the subservience to authority upon which domination systems depend. [4]

⤳

LABELING AND DIAGNOSIS is a catastrophic way to communicate. Telling other people what's wrong with them greatly reduces, almost to zero, the probability that we're going to get what we're after. [34]

> **Violence comes because of how we were educated, not because of our nature.** [8]

CAUSES OF VIOLENCE

VIOLENCE COMES BECAUSE of how we were educated, not because of our nature. [8]

⬬

THE MORE WE empathize with the pain that leads to violence, the less likelihood of violence. [14]

⬬

HOW COME ALL the violence? Well, we get educated. That's the problem. We get educated in a way that disconnects us from life's sweet flow. [19]

⬬

ALL YOU HAVE to do to teach people evil behavior is teach them a language that I call "jackal." Teach 'em to think there's a right and a wrong way to do everything. And then, if you want to make them really violent, teach them the concept of retributive justice, that's based on the murderous word *deserve*. Teach people that if you get one judgment that you're bad, you deserve to suffer. [19]

⬬

ANOTHER FORM OF violence: any attempt to get people to do things out of shame. . . . It involves using labels so that if people don't do what you want, you put labels on them like *lazy, inconsiderate,* or *stupid.* Any label that implies wrongness is a violent act. It's trying to get people to do things out of shame. [10]

⬬

AND PERHAPS THE worst violence we can use in the role of an educator—according to my values—is the violence of *"Amtssprache,"* which loosely translates into English as *"office talk"* or *"bureaucratese."* Why do I use that term? I borrow it from the Nazi war criminal

Adolph Eichmann. At his trial for war crimes in Jerusalem, Eichmann was asked, "Was it hard for you to send tens of thousands of people to their deaths?" Eichmann said: "To tell you the truth, it was easy. Our language made it easy." That response shocked his interviewer, and his interviewer said, "What language?" Eichmann said: "My fellow Nazi officers and I had our own name of our language. We called it '*amptssprache*.'" It's a language in which you deny responsibility for your actions. So if somebody asks you why you did what you did, you say "I had to." "Why did you have to?" "Superior's orders. Company policy. It's the law."

So here's classic *amptssprache*, the most dangerous words in the English language: *have to, can't*. And now here come some vulgar words. If you don't like vulgarity, close your ears: *should, must, ought*. [10]

~

VIOLENCE RESULTS WHEN people trick themselves into believing that their pain derives from other people and that consequently those people deserve to be punished. [34]

~

I SEE ALL anger as a result of life-alienating, violence-provoking thinking. At the core of all anger is a need that is not being fulfilled. [5]

~

THERE ARE TWO things that distinguish truly nonviolent actions from violent actions. First, there is no enemy in the nonviolent point of view. You don't see an enemy. Your thinking is clearly focused on protecting your needs. Second, your intention is not to make the other side suffer. [34]

~

SO IF YOU want to break peace and make life miserable, think of what's wrong with other people when they behave in a way you don't like. Use words that other people hear as criticism. You like to make life even more miserable? Think of what's wrong with you. But if you really like to be depressed, think of what other people think about you. You want to break even more peace and get even more miserable? Compare yourself to others. [29]

⤳

"YOU ARE THIS, you are that." Who wants to hear that? Boy, that makes it hard to enjoy being around people. So no, we never go up to the attic. There's cobwebs up there . . . dead rats. I mean it's horrible up there! And why go to someplace ugly, when if we see the truth, it's beautiful? The truth, to me, is really the feelings and needs. Go to the person's heart. [14]

⤳

CRITICISM, BLAME, PRAISE, and compliments are part of the thinking that I believe contributes to violence on our planet. And punishment and reward follow from that kind of thinking. That's why we have such a catastrophic judicial system. Our judicial system, called retributive justice, is all about . . . blaming and punishing. [21]

⤳

ANYTIME WE THINK of what we "are," we put ourselves into a casket. It's static thinking. But life is a process. [30]

⤳

WE NEED TO be thinking in a way that keeps us connected to life moment by moment. Every time we think of what we "are," we get disconnected from life. At the moment that I'm trying to think of what kind of person I am, I'm dead. [30]

DON'T "SHOULD" ON YOURSELF (OR OTHERS)

IN OUR LANGUAGE there is a word with enormous power to create shame and guilt. This violent word, which we commonly use to evaluate ourselves, is so deeply ingrained in our consciousness that many of us would have trouble imagining how to live without it. It is the word *should*, as in "I should have known better" or "I shouldn't have done that." Most of the time when we use this word with ourselves, we resist learning, because *should* implies that there is no choice. Human beings, when hearing any kind of demand, tend to resist because it threatens our autonomy—our strong need for choice. We have this reaction to tyranny even when it's internal tyranny in the form of a *should*. [5]

⤾

THE WORD *SHOULD* comes directly from this game of violence that implies there's a good and a bad, a *should* and a *shouldn't*. If you don't do the things you should do, you should be punished; if you do the right things, you should be rewarded. This creates enormous pain. [8]

⤾

DO YOU EVER hear an adult say, "I shouldn't smoke, I should give up smoking, I should lose weight." What do they do? They resist it. We weren't born to be slaves. *Should* is slave language. Human beings resist *shoulds*. [10]

⤾

ALL I HAVE to do is hear a *should* from inside or outside, and it takes all the joy out of doing it. So I try to never do anything I should do. . . . Do that which comes from this energy of how to make the world fun and learnable. Only come out of that energy. [18]

⤾

"
If we do anything
motivated through coercion,
everybody pays for it.
Unless it's play, don't do it. [10]
"

IF WE DO anything motivated through coercion, everybody pays for it. Unless it's play, don't do it. And it will be play, even it means cleaning floors or toilets, if there are no coercive aspects and we see how it enriches life. But tell yourself "I should do it," and you won't. Or you'll hate doing it. Don't do anything you should, have to, must. Don't do it if it isn't play. And it'll be play if it serves life, and you see how it serves life. It'll be play even if it involves hard work. [10]

~

IN HELPING PEOPLE get past the pain of *should*, we start by helping them become conscious of this thinking. Then we show people that this thinking is all a tragic expression of an unmet need. It means that you didn't meet a need of yours by doing what you did, and if you can identify the need of yours that wasn't met, you're far more likely to learn from it because you'll start to imagine how you could have better met the need without losing self-respect. So, we get them to identify the brutal language they're using to blame themselves, and then we teach them how to translate such language into *need* language.

At this point we show people how to connect empathically with what was alive in them when they did the behavior that they called a mistake. In other words, get clear what need they were trying to meet by doing it. [8]

~

WE WERE NOT meant to succumb to the dictates of *should* and *have to*, whether they come from outside or inside of ourselves. And if we do yield and submit to these demands, our actions arise from an energy that is devoid of life-giving joy. [5]

~

AVOID "SHOULDING" ON others and yourself! [34]

~

AS LONG AS I think I "should" do it, I'll resist it, even if I want very much to do it. [34]

∾

THE MOST DANGEROUS of all behaviors may consist of doing things "because we're supposed to." [34]

PART III

THE TWO PARTS OF NVC: EMPATHY AND EXPRESSION

I define empathy as our connection with what's alive in this person at this moment.[25]

6

THE GIFT OF EMPATHY

EMPATHY

EMPATHY IS WHERE we connect our attention, our consciousness; it's not what we say out loud. . . . I define empathy as our connection with what's alive in this person at this moment. [25]

❧

I DEFINE THE process of empathy as similar to the process of translating a foreign language into one's own language. In translating, the goal is to get at the exact meaning of the original message and then translate it into more familiar terms. Likewise, in offering empathy the goal is to translate the message being expressed into feelings and needs. [4]

❧

THE OTHER HALF of Nonviolent Communication . . . requires us to put on giraffe ears and learn how to hear any message that comes back at us as an expression of the other person's feelings and needs. Any message. So if the other person is silent, we don't hear the silence. With giraffe ears, we hear what this person might be feeling and needing behind the silence. If the other person says no, we don't hear it. We hear what the other person is feeling and needing. We have to guess. But we guess *human*. That's what Nonviolent Communication teaches us to do. No matter what message comes at us, we guess what this person might be feeling and needing. [10]

⤶

EMPATHY IS A respectful understanding of what others are experiencing. [5]

⤶

WE HAVE BEEN educated to think that there is something wrong with us. I want to suggest that you never, never, never hear what other people think about you. I predict you'll live longer, and you'll enjoy life more if you never hear what people think about you. Never take it personally. The recommendation I have is to learn to connect empathically with any message coming at us from other people. And Nonviolent Communication shows us a way of doing that. It shows us a way of seeing the beauty in the other person in any given moment, regardless of their behavior or their language. It requires connecting with the other person's feelings and needs at this moment, with what's alive in them. And when we do that, we're going to hear the other person singing a very beautiful song. [6]

⤶

IF YOU LEARN how to connect empathically with other people, you will hear that they are *always* singing a beautiful song. They are asking you to see the beautiful needs that are alive in them . . . this is what you will hear behind every message coming at you from another human being if you connect to the divine energy in that person at that moment. [8]

⤶

OFTEN, INSTEAD OF offering empathy, we have a strong urge to give advice or reassurance and to explain our own position or feeling. [34]

∽

MY OWN CHILDREN have taught me something important about advice. Never give advice unless you receive a request in writing signed by a lawyer, when it's your child. If it's one of my children I really need to triple check that they want advice, because it's almost my first reaction to skip the empathy and go directly to the advice. [18]

∽

A GIRAFFE NEVER tries to fix the other person's pain without a six-hour delay that gives the other person all the time they need to have their pain fully understood before you try to fix it. [22]

∽

OUR ABILITY TO offer empathy can allow us to stay vulnerable, defuse potential violence, help us hear the word *no* without taking it as a rejection, revive lifeless conversation, and even hear the feelings and needs expressed through silence. [34]

∽

EMPATHY ALLOWS US to re-perceive our world in a new way and move forward. [34]

∽

TIME AND AGAIN I have witnessed people transcend the paralyzing effects of psychological pain when they have sufficient contact with someone who can hear them empathically. As listeners, we don't need insights into psychological dynamics or training in psychotherapy. What is essential is our ability to be present to what's really going on

> **Empathy allows us to re-perceive our world in a new way and move forward.** [34]

within—to the unique feelings and needs a person is experiencing in that very moment. [5]

⌇

THE INTENT IS what's important; not that we guess right, but that we be sincerely interested in connecting with the person's needs. [22]

⌇

PEOPLE IN PAIN aren't generally conscious of what they want. I start with the assumption that they want empathy. But what form? Silent? Some people just like me to . . . be there and not say a word for a while. So I try to guess what form they would like it [empathy] in. Do they want it in this moment verbally, or silently? [18]

⌇

SOMETIMES OUR EMPATHY can be communicated nonverbally and no verbal reflection is necessary. When we are fully present to what is alive in others, we wear a different expression than when we are mentally analyzing the person or thinking of what we are going to say next. However empathy is expressed, it touches a very deep need in human beings to feel that someone else can truly hear them, and hear them nonjudgmentally. [4]

⌇

THERE ARE NO infallible guidelines regarding when to paraphrase, but as a rule of thumb, it is safe to assume that speakers expressing intensely emotional messages would appreciate our reflecting these back to them. When we ourselves are talking, we can make it easier for the listener if we clearly signify when we want or don't want our words to be reflected back to us. [5]

⌇

TO EMPATHIZE WE don't have to know anything about the past. I just have to connect with what's alive in her now, as a result of what happened in the past. I could guess. But empathy is to connect with what's alive right now. [19]

⤳

IF WE ARE sincerely trying to connect with the divine energy in another human being . . . that shows the other person that no matter how they communicate with us, we care about what's alive in them. When a person trusts that, we're well on our way to making a connection in which everybody's needs can get met. [8]

⤳

WITH GIRAFFE EARS on, we might hear different things, but if we are really sincerely trying to hear what that person is feeling, we show it in our eyes. We have different eyes when we are sincerely trying to connect with what's alive in somebody than when we're hearing a criticism or making one. [26]

⤳

WHEN WE ARE really directly connected with the needs of others—at the point at which we understand their needs—we are not really in touch with any feelings within ourselves, because our full attention is on the other person. [9]

⤳

SO WHATEVER WORDS I use are not as important as where am I connected. The words are not empathy. The connection is the empathy. When this person feels that I'm connected . . . that's empathy. Not when I think I'm giving them empathy. . . . Whatever words get me there, I'll use. [25]

⤳

WE NEVER HAVE the same feelings that another person has, because that feeling is unique to this moment in time. So empathy requires that we see this person's feelings at this moment in time as a newborn infant. It's never been before and it will never be again. I have never had the feeling that this person is feeling at this moment. I've had feelings that I may intellectually identify as close to it, but I have never felt that person's feeling. Only they have. [18]

↬

WITH THESE [GIRAFFE] ears on, you cannot hear silence. If the other person just looks down at the floor, and you have these ears on, it's a very loud message. You hear what are they feeling, what needs are creating their feelings. [21]

↬

ONE OF THE hardest messages for many of us to empathize with is silence. This is especially true when we've expressed ourselves vulnerably and need to know how others are reacting to our words. At such times, it's easy to project our worst fears onto the lack of response and forget to connect with the feelings and needs being expressed through the silence. [5]

↬

I TRY NEVER to connect, even verbally, a person's pain to forces outside themselves. I'm gonna connect the pain immediately to a need. [25]

↬

WE MAY FIND ourselves being defensive or apologetic, instead of empathetic, in the presence of those we identify as our "superiors." [5]

↬

THE NUMBER ONE rule of our training is empathy before education. [34]

THE MORE ANOTHER person's behavior is not in harmony with my own needs, the more I empathize with them and their needs, the more likely I am to get my own needs met. [34]

∽

THE BEST WAY I can get understanding from another person is to give this person the understanding too. If I want them to hear my needs and feelings, I first need to empathize. [34]

∽

IF I ASK the other person something about what they've just said, and I am met with "That's a stupid question," I hear them expressing a need in the form of a judgment of me, and proceed to guess what that need might be. [31]

∽

THE MORE WE connect with the feelings and needs behind their words, the less frightening it is to open up to other people. [5]

∽

WE NEED EMPATHY to give empathy. [5]

∽

IT IS IMPOSSIBLE for us to give something to another if we don't have it ourselves. Likewise, if we find ourselves unable or unwilling to empathize despite our efforts, it is usually a sign that we are too starved for empathy to be able to offer it to others. [5]

∽

IT REALLY HELPS me to be part of a giraffe community of people that I can call on when I get stuck and I'm not in touch with what's going on in me that's keeping me from being able to connect with this other person. [22]

⤷

WHEN WE SENSE ourselves being defensive or unable to empathize, we need to (1) stop, breathe, give ourselves empathy; (2) scream nonviolently; or (3) take time out. [5]

⤷

DON'T TRY TO empathize with other people until you have gotten to the point of self-forgiveness. [18]

⤷

WE ALL NEED daily empathy, and we can give it to ourselves, but . . . I think there's a quality that comes from getting it from other people that's very powerful. [19]

⤷

IT IS A poignant experience to receive concrete evidence that someone is empathically connected to us. [5]

⤷

I THINK WE all need an empathy team. [19]

⤷

EMPATHY IS LIKE riding on a wave; it's about getting in touch with a certain energy. But the energy is a divine energy that's alive in every person, at every moment. [8]

THE POWER OF PRESENCE

EMPATHY LIES IN our ability to be present without opinion. [34]

∽

WHAT DOES EMPATHY mean? Empathy is mostly presence. Presence. Martin Buber describes this as the most precious gift one human being can give to another. Our presence. Because it means, at this moment, we bring nothing from the past to this moment. This means all of our prior images of this person, all of our psychological training, all of that must be left out. To be present, to just see what is alive in this person at this moment, free from anything we bring in from the past. [26]

∽

EMPATHY WITH OTHERS occurs only when we have successfully shed all preconceived ideas and judgments about them. [5]

∽

ONE COMPONENT OF empathy is to be fully present to what the other person is currently feeling and needing, and not losing that through a fog of diagnosis or interpretation. This requires that our minds not wander off on paths of analysis while we seem to be listening to the person before us. [4]

∽

NOW, WE CAN be present to many things. So what are we present to? In empathy we're present to what's alive in the person at this moment. And the best way I know to do that is to connect with what they're feeling and what they're needing. [26]

∽

EMPATHY FIRST OF all requires this presence—full presence to what's alive in the other person at this moment. Next, empathy requires focus on what is alive in them now, which to me means what are they feeling at this moment and what are they needing. That's the closest I know to getting in touch with what's alive in somebody. [18]

↜

THE FIRST STEP to empathic connection is what Martin Buber calls the most precious gift one human being can give to another: presence. . . . This is a hard gift to give to somebody, because it means that I can bring nothing in from the past. Even a diagnosis I've had of this person in the past will get in the way of empathy. [2]

↜

THIS BEING FULLY present also requires that we clear our consciousness of whatever preconceived ideas or judgments we may have been harboring about the person speaking. I would not want this to sound like I am advocating suppressing or repressing one's feelings. It is more a matter of being so focused on the feelings of the speaker that our own reactions do not intrude. [4]

↜

WITH EMPATHY WE don't direct, we follow. Don't *do* something, just be there. Your presence is the most precious gift you can give to another human being. [10]

↜

YOU SEE, IF we're mentally trying to understand the other person, we're not present with them in this moment. [8]

↜

SOMETIMES IT'S PRETTY obvious what the person is feeling and needing; we don't have to say it. They'll feel it from our eyes whether we are really trying to connect with them. Notice this does not require that we agree with the other person. It doesn't mean we have to like what they're saying. It means that we give them this precious gift of our presence, to be present at this moment to what's alive in this person and that we are interested in that, sincerely interested. Not as a psychological technique, but because we want to connect with the divine energy in that person at this moment. [6]

⤺

THE PRESENCE THAT empathy requires is not easy to maintain. . . . Instead of offering empathy, we tend instead to give advice or reassurance and to explain our own position or feeling. Empathy, on the other hand, requires us to focus full attention on the other person's message. We give to others the time and space they need to express themselves fully and to feel understood. [5]

⤺

BELIEVING WE HAVE to "fix" situations and make others feel better prevents us from being present. [5]

⤺

CLINICAL TRAINING IN psychoanalysis has a deficit. It teaches how to sit and think about what a person is saying and how to interpret it intellectually, but not how to be fully present to this person. [34]

⤺

MARTIN BUBER, THE Israeli philosopher and psychotherapist, says that presence is the most powerful gift one person can give to another. A powerful gift and a precious gift. When we give this gift to others— this gift of our presence—it is a major component of healing. [31]

EMPATHY VS SYMPATHY

WITH EMPATHY, I'M fully with them, and not full of them—that's sympathy. [34]

THE KEY INGREDIENT of empathy is presence: we are wholly present with the other party and what they are experiencing. This quality of presence distinguishes empathy from either mental understanding or sympathy. While we may choose at times to sympathize with others by feeling their feelings, it's helpful to be aware that during the moment we are offering sympathy, we are not empathizing. [5]

EMPATHIC CONNECTION IS an understanding of the heart in which we see the beauty in the other person, the divine energy in the other person, the life that's alive in them. We connect with it. The goal isn't intellectually understanding it, the goal is empathically connecting with it. It doesn't mean we have to feel the same feelings as the other person. That's sympathy, when we feel sad that another person is upset. It doesn't mean we have to have the same feelings; it means we are *with* the other person. This quality of understanding requires one of the most precious gifts one human being can give to another: our presence in the moment. [8]

SYMPATHY, EMPATHY—LET'S get clear about the difference. If I have strong feelings in me, just being conscious of them is sympathy, not empathy. . . . Remember a time when you had a pain in your body, maybe a headache or a toothache, and you got into a good book? What happened to the pain? You weren't aware of it. It was there, I mean the physical condition hadn't changed, but you weren't home. You were out visiting: That's empathy. You were visiting the book.

With empathy, we're with the other person. That doesn't mean we feel their feelings. We're with them while they are feeling their feelings. Now, if I take my mind away from the person for one second, I may notice I have strong feelings. If so, I don't try to push my feelings down. They tell me I'm not with the other person. I'm home again. So I say to myself, "Go back to them."

However, if my pain is too great, I can't empathize. So I might say, "I'm in so much pain right now hearing some things you've said—I'm not able to listen. Could we give me a few moments to deal with that so that I can go back to hearing you?"

It's important not to mix up empathy and sympathy, because when this person is in pain and then I say, "Oh, I understand how you feel and I feel so sad about that," I take the flow away from them, bring their attention over to me. [2]

⌇

AT THE MOMENT we say to someone, "I feel sad to hear you are in such pain," we are not empathically connecting with the other person's pain. We are expressing the pain we feel that was stimulated by the other's pain. That is sympathy. A sympathetic response can also be a gift to the other person if our timing is right. If we respond sympathetically after we have connected empathically, this can deepen our connection with the other person. However, if we respond with sympathy when the other person needs empathy, this can disconnect us. [4]

EMPATHY VS UNDERSTANDING

INTELLECTUAL UNDERSTANDING BLOCKS empathy. [34]

⌇

SEE, THAT'S A mistake many people make, that if we empathize it's going to sound like we're agreeing with the behavior. Condoning it. Or that we're going to put up with it. No, empathy means that we can understand that everything each human being does is perfect for them to do. [14]

⤳

EMPATHY, OF COURSE, is a special kind of understanding. It's not an understanding of the head where we just mentally understand what another person says. It's something far deeper and more precious than that. Empathic connection is an understanding of the heart where we see the beauty in the other person, the divine energy in the other person, the life that's alive in them. We connect with it. We don't mentally understand it, we connect with it. [6]

⤳

IF WE'RE MENTALLY trying to understand the other person, we're not present with them in this moment. We're sitting there analyzing them, but we're not with them. So, empathic connection involves *connecting with what is alive in the other person at this moment.* [6]

⤳

MOST PEOPLE THINK you have to understand the past to get healing. And that you have to tell the story to get the understanding. They mix up intellectual understanding with empathy. Empathy is where the healing comes from. Telling the story does give intellectual understanding about why the person did it, but that's not empathy, and it doesn't do any healing. In fact, retelling the story deepens the pain. It's like reliving the pain again. [2]

⤳

EMPATHY SHOWS WE have no moralistic judgment of the person for what they're doing. [28]

EMPATHY ISN'T AGREEMENT

EVERYTHING THAT EACH of us does is perfect. If we empathize, we'll see that. But that doesn't mean that we want to tolerate that. It means we have a respectful understanding that for that person at that place and time, that's the best they can do. So that's all empathy means, is looking at the person with those eyes. Having understood that, that doesn't mean that we have to like it or put up with it. [14]

⇌

NOTICE THIS DOESN'T require that we agree with the other person. It doesn't mean we have to like what they're saying. It means that we give them this precious gift of our presence, to be present at this moment to what's alive in them, that we are interested, sincerely interested in that. We don't do it as a psychological technique but because we want to connect with the beauty in the person at this moment. [8]

⇌

THE MOST POWERFUL opening gambit that I know of, whether it's within social change or if I'm working with people in prisons who've done things that I'm very frightened of, the most powerful thing I can do is to connect empathically with the person who is doing what I don't like in a way that I sincerely show them that I have no judgment of them for doing it. It's the most powerful thing that I can do, but it requires a lot of work, because it requires getting all enemy images out of my head. It requires me being conscious that I'm not out to change the other person. I'm out to create a connection that will allow everyone's needs to get met. [3]

A FREQUENTLY RAISED concern about empathy is "Wouldn't the student think that you are condoning his thoughts and feelings if you reflect them back that way?" In response I try to make it clear that there is a difference between empathic understanding and agreement. I can show understanding of a student's feelings and needs without implying that I agree, condone, or even like his feelings and needs. [4]

WHAT'S ENOUGH EMPATHY?

DID YOU COUNT to a million before shifting the focus from the other person to yourself? Count to one million slowly before reacting after empathizing. Because I might have just been about to get into something really deep, and if you go that quickly to your reaction it looks like you're using empathy as a technique. It's as if the whole time, you're just waiting for me to be finished so you can get your two cents worth in. Now I don't trust your empathy. So, count to a million before you switch away from empathic connection with the other person. [3]

~

TWO SIGNS INDICATE that speakers may be ready to move to their requests. First, when people have had the empathy they need at a given time, they feel relieved, and we can usually sense this relief. Another more obvious sign is that they stop talking. However, it doesn't hurt to ask them, "Is there more you would like to say?" before moving to their requests. [4]

~

I RECOMMEND ALLOWING others the opportunity to fully express themselves before turning our attention to solutions or requests for relief. When we proceed too quickly to what people might be requesting, we may not convey our genuine interest in their feelings and needs; instead, they may get the impression that we're in a hurry to either be free of them or to fix their problem. Furthermore, an initial message is often like the tip of an iceberg; it may be followed by as yet unexpressed, but related— and often more powerful—feelings. By maintaining our attention on what's going on within others, we offer them a chance to fully explore and express their interior selves. We would stem this flow if we were to shift attention too quickly either to their request or to our own desire to express ourselves. [5]

～

I STAY IN a dialogue until I feel that we're at the bottom of what's really alive in this person right now. Now, it's not too easy to know when you really have reached this point. We have two clues that can give us a little bit of data. One, when the person really feels understood we'll feel it in our body. There is a certain release of tension that happens when any human being gets the understanding at this moment that they needed. Anybody in the room will usually feel it in their body as well. It's an "ahhhhhhh." The person usually stops at that point; they don't just keep going on. So, those two clues may indicate that they've had the understanding they need to move down to the request. Now, it's always good to be slow and conservative before we move the attention away from them back to ourselves. To say something like, "Is there more you want me to hear about this?" Give them plenty of space to explore all that's going on in them. [3]

SELF-EMPATHY

SELF-EMPATHY IN NVC means checking in with your own feelings and needs. [34]

～

IN A SENSE, getting our mind to go blank is a very important part of Nonviolent Communication. And you do that by just observing the jackal

> "Self-empathy in NVC
> means checking in with your
> own feelings and needs. [34]

show that's going on inside. Just to see it. It's not us. It's programmed into us; it's like a movie was put into our head. Just see that, and then come back to life. . . . We see what's going on in our head, but behind it we connect; what need of mine is there? [12]

⬲

SELF-EMPATHY, FOR me, is getting connected at any given moment with what I'm feeling and to connect my feelings to my needs. Those two things: our empathic connection is with feelings and needs. So, if I say to myself, "What a stupid thing to do!" Then I just hear that I think that was stupid. Hearing my thoughts is like taking a bath with your clothes on. They're not really getting down to the bare facts. The bare facts are feelings and needs. [19]

⬲

WHEN PEOPLE CAN practice self-empathy, they are much better able to learn from their limitations without losing self-respect—without feeling guilty or depressed.

In fact, I would say that if we're not able to empathize with ourselves, it's going to be very hard to do it with other people. If we still think when we make a mistake that there's something wrong with us, then how are we not going to think there's something wrong with other people for doing what they do? When we can empathize with ourselves and really stay connected to our true self in a life-enriching way, we can hear or sense which needs we're not meeting by our actions, at which point we also can see which needs we were trying to meet by doing what we just did. When our awareness is on our needs, we're much better able to meet our needs without losing self-respect, and we're also better able to avoid judging others for what they say or do. [8]

⬲

TRANSLATE ALL SELF-JUDGMENTS into self-empathy. [34]

7

EXPRESSING YOURSELF USING NVC

EXPRESSION

BECAUSE WE ARE called to reveal our deepest feelings and needs, we may sometimes find it challenging to express ourselves in NVC. Self-expression becomes easier, however, after we empathize with others, because we will then have touched their humanness and realized the common qualities we share. The more we connect with the feelings and needs behind their words, the less frightening it is to open up to other people. The situations where we are the most reluctant to express vulnerability are often those where we want to maintain a "tough image" for fear of losing authority or control. [5]

↪

WE'VE BEEN EDUCATED to see our needs as kind of dirty, dependent, egotistical, unnecessary, not important. So it's very hard for us to get up the courage to express them. When we do finally express them, we do it out of fear, anxiety, guilt, and anger. That stimulates a reaction . . . that strengthens our belief that our needs are something bad. [19]

THE MORE DIRECTLY we can connect our feelings to our own needs, the easier it is for others to respond to us compassionately. [5]

⤳

WE'LL ALWAYS KNOW that the other person heard us when we express our needs, because they'll have the look on their face of a little child talking to Santa Claus. If they don't have that look, they didn't hear. [16]

⤳

WE'VE GOT TO be prepared, anytime we express ourselves vulnerably, we have to be prepared to empathically deal with what comes back. [31]

⤳

IF YOU CAN'T get to what you want in forty words or less, you're likely to get a lot of what you don't want. See, all of this, this part, what's alive in you, is observation, feelings, and needs. You can say that in forty words. If you're doing more than forty words, you're probably talking about thoughts, justifying, explaining in ways that are not helpful. [12]

⤳

WHEN YOU WANT a connection with people about emotional issues express what's in your heart, your feelings, your needs in about thirty words and then take the rest of the forty to make a present request. Human beings in an emotional situation—it's asking a big gift from them to give you their full attention for the forty words. [22]

⤳

LET ME TELL you what many people are afraid will happen if they open up and reveal themselves. When they reveal honestly what's alive in them and what would make life more wonderful, many people are afraid they're going to get a free diagnosis from the other person. The other person is going to tell them what's wrong with them for having these feelings, needs, and requests. They're afraid they'll hear things about how they're too sensitive, needy, or demanding. This can happen, of course. We live in a world where people think that way, so if we are really open and honest, we might get back a diagnosis. Good news, though! Nonviolent Communication prepares us to deal with any response that might come back. Other people are afraid of silence. . . . Many other people are afraid of a tiny two-letter word: *no*.[8]

〰

MY BELIEF IS that, whenever we say something to another person, we are requesting something in return. It may simply be an empathic connection—a verbal or nonverbal acknowledgment . . . that our words have been understood. Or we may be requesting honesty: we wish to know the listener's honest reaction to our words. Or we may be requesting an action that we hope would fulfill our needs. The clearer we are on what we want back from the other person, the more likely it is that our needs will be met.[5]

〰

AS WE KNOW, the message we send is not always the message that's received. We generally rely on verbal cues to determine whether our message has been understood to our satisfaction. If, however, we're uncertain that it has been received as intended, we need to be able to clearly request a response that tells us how the message was heard so as to be able to correct any misunderstanding. On some occasions, a simple question like, "Is that clear?" will suffice. At other times, we need more than "Yes, I understood you," to feel confident that we've been truly understood. At such times, we might ask others to reflect back in their own words what they heard us say. We then have the opportunity to restate parts of our message to address any discrepancy or omission we might have noticed in their reflection.[5]

ANYTIME THE LOOK in the other person's eyes is not the look of a little child receiving a gift from Santa Claus, we know they didn't hear us. If we spoke in pure giraffe, we will see in the other person's eyes, the eyes of a child receiving a gift. [22]

 ⸝

NONVIOLENT COMMUNICATION REQUIRES us living in the moment, now. And to be clear, what we want now, back from the other person when we speak. So we've got to end, when we're expressing pain, on a clear, present request. [26]

 ⸝

THE NUMBER ONE reason that we don't get our needs met: we don't express them. We express judgments. If we do express needs, the number two reason we don't get our needs met—we don't make clear requests. [34]

 ⸝

FIRST, WE DON'T know how to express our needs to begin with, and second, if we do, we forget to put a clear request after it, or we use vague words like appreciate, listen, recognize, know, be real, and stuff like that. [34]

 ⸝

IF WE SIMPLY express the need without the request, it often leaves the other person in a position [of] either not being clear what we want, or with the idea that we expect them to know what we want them to do about it. [31]

 ⸝

WHENEVER . . . YOU'RE NOT clear what you're wanting back, don't expect to have a productive conversation. You will have people talking at each other, but not with each other. [12]

IT IS ESPECIALLY important when we are addressing a group to be clear about the kind of understanding or honesty we want back after we've expressed ourselves. When we are not clear about the response we'd like, we may initiate unproductive conversations that end up satisfying no one's needs. [5]

⤳

WHEN WE ADDRESS a group without being clear what we are wanting back, unproductive discussions will often follow. However, if even one member of a group is conscious of the importance of clearly requesting the response that is desired, he or she can extend this consciousness to the group. [5]

⤳

WHEN WE'RE NOT clear what we want back from our listener we usually use about 90 percent more words than is necessary. If we want something, but we're not clear what it is, then we think that somehow by talking forever we're going to get it. [27]

⤳

CONVERSATIONS OFTEN DRAG on and on, fulfilling no one's needs, because it is unclear whether the initiator of the conversation has gotten what she or he wanted. In India, when people have received the response they want in conversations they have initiated, they say "*bas*" (pronounced "bus"). This means, "You need not say more. I feel satisfied and am now ready to move on to something else." Though we lack such a word in our own language, we can benefit from developing and promoting "bas-consciousness" in all our interactions. [5]

⤳

WHEN WE EXPRESS our needs indirectly through the use of evaluations, interpretations, and images, others are likely to hear criticism. When people hear anything that sounds like criticism, they tend to invest their energy in self-defense or counterattack. It's important that when we address somebody that we're clear what we want back. [34]

⮌

EMOTIONAL LIBERATION INVOLVES stating clearly what we need in a way that communicates we are equally concerned that the needs of others be fulfilled. NVC is designed to support us in relating at this level. [5]

BEING ASSERTIVE

NVC IS A very assertive language. We can be very loud and clear about what we feel, what our needs are, what we want from the other person, but we're very assertive without doing two things which turn assertiveness into violence. In NVC we assert ourselves but without criticizing the other. So, we say nothing in the language of NVC that in any way implies that the other person is ever wrong. And by wrong I mean about a thousand different things, inappropriate, selfish, insensitive, in fact any word that classifies or categorizes what the other person is.

In NVC we learn how to be very assertive about saying what's going on in us, and we also have the wonderful art when we speak NVC of very assertively telling people what we would like them to do, but we present this to them as a request and not as a demand. Because at the moment people hear from our lips anything that sounds like a criticism or a demand, or it sounds somehow to them like we don't value their needs equal to our needs—when the other person gets that impression from us, that we are only out to get our way, we lose, because then the other person has less energy to sincerely consider our needs. Most of their energy will go into defensiveness or resistance.

We want to be very assertive when we speak NVC in a way that gives the other person our assertiveness as a gift that reveals nakedly what's going on in us, clearly tells us what we would like from them. [1]

8

DIFFICULT EMOTIONS:
ANGER, DEPRESSION, GUILT, AND SHAME

WHEN OUR NEEDS aren't getting met, we're frustrated. But when we get angry, guilty, depressed, or shamed, we're not in touch with our needs. We're up in our heads, analyzing. [27]

↜

WHAT ARE THESE four wonderful feelings that tell us we are, at that moment, thinking in a way that is creating violence on the planet? Anger. Depression. Guilt. Shame. Those feelings are created by a very violent way of thinking. [26]

↜

ANGER, DEPRESSION, GUILT, and shame tell us we've lost connection with life. We're not connected to our needs. We're up in our head, thinking in a way that creates great pain on our planet. So become conscious of the thinking, and then ask yourself, "What need is at the root of those thoughts?" [19]

↜

THE THINKING THAT makes us feel angry, depressed, guilty, and ashamed—the thinking that's going on in our heads at that moment—is a tragic, suicidal expression of an unmet need or unmet needs. There are whole cultures that do not feel anger, depression, guilt, and shame. They're not taught to think in the way that creates those feelings. They have strong emotions. But not anger, depression, guilt, and shame. [19]

WHEN WE ARE in touch with our unmet need, we never feel shame, guilt, self-anger, or the depression that we feel when we think that what we did was wrong. We feel sadness, deep sadness, sometimes frustration, but never depression, guilt, anger, or shame. Those four feelings tell us we are making moralistic judgments at the moment we are feeling those feelings. [2]

OUR FEELINGS ARE caused by one of two things: Mother Nature, or our thinking. Mother Nature is responsible for sadness, loneliness, frustration, because those feelings directly connect to needs that aren't getting met. But feelings like anger, depression, guilt, and shame, are a result of a combination of two factors: Mother Nature—our needs aren't getting met—but our thinking is not need-connected, it's up in our head, playing the game of judgments. [19]

WE DON'T WANT to get rid of the pain if it's need-connected. That's nature's way of mobilizing us to get the need met. But if it's any of those other feelings—anger, guilt, shame—if the tension is coming out of that, then we need to get more connected to life by empathizing with the need that's being expressed through these inner messages. [15]

SO SOME OF us look inward and choose to take things personally. If we do, we'll spend a good deal of our life feeling guilty, shamed, and depressed. If we judge others, we'll spend a good deal of our life being angry. And some of us are very talented. At one moment we can take in a statement like this and think, "Oh, I must be a bad teacher to have somebody talk to me that way," and we feel guilty or shamed, and then we flip around and get angry. We go through life vacillating between angry, guilty, shamed, depressed, angry, guilty, shamed, depressed.

Incidentally, those are very valuable feelings to a person using Nonviolent Communication: the feelings of anger, depression, guilt, and shame. Why are they valuable? All of those feelings tell us that we are dead. We're dead in this sense: we're cut off from where our attention really needs to be to see the beauty in ourselves and other people. And where do I suggest we place our attention? On the most important ingredient of Nonviolent Communication: needs. [10]

DEPRESSION

DEPRESSION IS THE reward we get for being "good." [34]

⤳

IT'S THIS KIND of thinking that makes us depressed: what we tell ourselves about ourselves. We judge ourselves in a way we've been trained to judge people. These judgments that imply badness, wrongness, inferiority, abnormality—that creates the depression. [31]

⤳

WE OFTEN EDUCATE ourselves through guilt, shame, and other forms of violent, coercive tactics. We know we're doing that. How do we know that we are educating ourselves in a violent way?

Three feelings will tell us: depression, guilt, and shame. I think we feel depressed a good deal of the time, not because we're ill or something is wrong with us, but because we have been taught to educate ourselves with moralistic judgments, to blame ourselves. [8]

～

WHEN WE ARE depressed, our thinking blocks us from being aware of our needs, and then being able to take action to meet our needs. [34]

～

WHEN WE HAVE a judgmental dialogue going on within, we become alienated from what we are needing and cannot then act to meet those needs. Depression is indicative of a state of alienation from our own needs. [5]

～

NVC ENHANCES INNER communication by helping us translate negative internal messages into feelings and needs. Our ability to distinguish our own feelings and needs and to empathize with them can free us from depression. [34]

～

YOU CANNOT BE depressed when you're connected to your needs. So I work with a lot of very depressed people, and I say "What needs of yours are not getting met?" "I'm a failure." See the difference between the question I asked and the answer I got? I asked for what needs of yours aren't getting met—"I'm a failure." As long as you think of what you "are," get used to being depressed. [19]

～

"

Our ability to distinguish our own
feelings and needs and to empathize
with them can free us from
depression. [34]

"

DEPRESSION, I BELIEVE, is created by jackal thinking directed inward. So I would much rather teach them giraffe, because my experience is that that will help the most. And to teach this person that there's something wrong with them that requires chemicals, I think contributes to the problem. Because they're already jackaling themselves—that's why they're depressed—and now they get convinced of that and somebody gives them drugs. [14]

꼬

I DON'T THINK anybody really knows whether some people who are depressed, it might be chemical. So I don't want to rule out that possibility. All I'm telling you is, when families come to me, I say "Whether that's so or not, I don't know. If you want to take the medication . . . that'd be your decision. But I'll approach it as though it's jackal thinking that's creating the problem." Doesn't seem to me it hurts anything to learn giraffe; it's not toxic or anything. [14]

ANGER

ANGER CAN BE a wonderful wake-up call to help you understand what you need and what you value. [34]

꼬

WHEN YOU'RE ANGRY, it brings many aspects of the NVC process into sharp focus, helping you see the difference between NVC and other forms of communication. [9]

꼬

ANGER IS NOT the problem. It's the thinking that's going on in us when we're angry that's the problem. [18]

꼬

ON THE SUBJECT of anger, that's a good feeling to teach us Nonviolent Communication, because anger tells us that we are disconnected from our needs, the central part of Nonviolent Communication. Anger tells us we're thinking in a way that creates violence on the planet. [31]

ↄ

ANGER IS A signal that you're distracted by judgmental or punitive thinking, and that some precious need of yours is being ignored. [34]

ↄ

I BELIEVE THAT all anger is a result of thinking. Jackal (judgmental) thinking. And when people are angry, I'm suggesting they're not fully in contact with their unmet needs. Most of their energy is going into analyzing their environment. Most of their energy isn't on their own needs. [13]

ↄ

MY ANGER IS valuable. It's really a blessing. When I'm angry I know I need to slow down, look at what I'm telling myself. Translate the judgments that are making me angry and get in touch with my needs. [2]

ↄ

USE ANGER AS a wake-up call to unmet needs. [34]

ↄ

ANGER IS ALWAYS justified in the sense that it's the inevitable result of life-alienated, violence-provocative thinking. [2]

ↄ

SO IN NVC we are interested in using the anger in ways that help us to get at the needs that are not being fulfilled within ourselves, that are at the root of our anger. [9]

〜

NONVIOLENT COMMUNICATION REQUIRES us to be conscious that all the thinking that's going on inside us that makes us angry is a tragic expression of our needs. [28]

〜

THIS IS THE natural function of emotions, to stimulate us to get our needs met. But anger is stimulated by a diversion. We are not in touch with the needs that would naturally motivate us to want to get our needs met. The anger is created, as I've said, by thinking about the wrongness of others, which transfers this energy away from seeking to get the need met, into an energy designed to blame and punish other people. [9]

〜

WHEN OUR FULL attention is on our needs, it's impossible to be angry. No matter what the person is doing to you, you cannot be angry if your full attention is either on your need or the other person's need. [22]

〜

IF WE ARE to manage anger in ways that are in harmony with the principles of NVC, it's important for us to be conscious of this key distinction: *I feel as I do because I am telling myself thoughts about the other person's actions that imply wrongness on their part.* Such thoughts take the form of judgments such as, "I think the person is selfish, I think the person is rude, or lazy, or manipulating people, and they shouldn't do that." Such thoughts take either the form of direct judgment of others or indirect judgments expressed through such things as, "I'm judging this person as thinking only they have something worth saying." In these latter expressions, it's implicit that we think what they're doing isn't right.

Now that's important, because if I think this other person is making me feel this way, it's going to be hard for me not to imagine punishing them. We show people it's never what the other person does; it's how you see it; how you interpret it. [9]

The Cause of Anger

THE CAUSE OF anger lies in our thinking—in thoughts of blame and judgment. [34]

⤺

WE ARE NEVER angry because of what others say or do; it is a result of our own "should" thinking. [34]

⤺

WHENEVER WE ARE angry, we are finding fault—we are choosing to play God by judging or blaming the other person for being wrong or deserving punishment. I would like to suggest that this is the cause of anger. Even if we are not initially conscious of it, the cause of anger is located in our own thinking. [5]

⤺

THE KIND OF thinking that leads us to be angry is thinking that implies that people deserve to suffer for what they've done. In other words, I'm talking about the moralistic judgments we make of other people that imply wrongness, irresponsibility, or inappropriateness. At their root, all of these kinds of judgments imply that people shouldn't have done what they did, and they deserve some form of condemnation or punishment for doing it. [9]

⤺

I SEE ALL anger as a result of life-alienating, violence-provoking thinking. At the core of all anger is a need that is not being fulfilled.

Thus anger can be valuable if we use it as an alarm clock to wake us up—to realize we have a need that isn't being met and that we are thinking in a way that makes it unlikely to be met. [5]

∽

I KNOW THAT anytime there's anger in a person's heart, there's a *should* in their head. That's the cause of anger. And we've been given—since that's such an important word, *should*—in the jackal culture, we have about a thousand variations of the word *should*. *Shouldn't*. For example, like *selfish*. *Inconsiderate, inappropriate, freedom fighter, terrorist*. Those are all variations on the word *should*, and that's the cause of the anger. [19]

∽

ANGER IS A result of life-alienating thinking that is disconnected from needs. It indicates that we have moved up to our head to analyze and judge somebody rather than focus on which of our needs are not getting met. [5]

∽

THE FIRST STEP in handling our anger using NVC is to be conscious that *the stimulus, or trigger, of our anger is not the cause of our anger.* That is to say that it isn't simply what people do that makes us angry, but it's something within us that responds to what they do that is really the cause of the anger. This requires us to be able to separate the trigger from the cause. [9]

∽

IN NVC, WHENEVER we feel angry, we recommend saying to ourselves, "I'm feeling angry because I am telling myself _____," and then to look for the kind of life-alienated thinking going on inside our head that is the cause of our anger. [9]

∽

NOW, THIS IS very hard for many of us to keep straight: to not mix up the trigger, or stimulus, of our anger with the cause of our anger. The reason that that's not easy for us is that we may have been educated by people who use guilt as a primary form of trying to motivate us. When you want to use guilt as a way of manipulating people, you need to confuse them into thinking that the trigger is the cause of the feeling. In other words, if you want to use guilt with somebody, you need to communicate in a way that indicates that your pain is being caused simply by what they do. In other words, their behavior is not simply the stimulus of your feelings; it's the cause of your feelings. [9]

WE TRY TO get people to see that when you're angry, it's because your consciousness is under the influence of the kind of language we all learned: that the other side is evil or bad in some way. It's that thinking that is the cause of anger. When that thinking is going on, we show people not how to push it down and deny the anger or deny the thinking, but to transform it into a language of life, into a language in which you are much more likely to create peace between yourself and whoever acted in the way that stimulated your anger.

We talk first about how to get conscious of this internalized thinking that's making you angry and how to transform that into what needs of yours have not been met by what the other person has done, and then how to proceed from that consciousness to create peace again between you and that person. [9]

WHEN YOU CAN'T see any good reason for why a person does something, you pay for it, because every human being, everything they do, is for a good reason. The same reason: to meet a need. It's the best way they knew to meet a need of theirs at that time. When you hear that, you can't be angry. It's not possible. You can only be angry when, instead of empathically connecting with people, you judge them. And we pay for it when we judge people. Even if we don't say it out loud, we pay for it. [12]

IF YOU DEFINE being alive as having a shot of adrenaline in your system, then anger makes you feel alive. But I define being alive as being connected to life. And to me, life is needs in action. Any living phenomenon has needs: Trees have needs. Dogs have needs, flies have needs, human beings have needs. Anything alive. So to me, being alive is to be connected to life, to needs. And anger tells me I'm disconnected from my needs. [19]

Managing Your Own Anger

WHENEVER YOU GET angry, I would suggest, first of all, shut up. Don't say or do anything. Instead, quick, put on a giraffe hat. Now. Next step, when you have the giraffe hat on, just see what's going on in your head that's making you angry. So, be conscious that it is never what the other person did that makes you angry. [19]

⌇

WHATEVER YOU SAY while you're angry is very unlikely to get you what you want for reasons you won't have to pay for later. [19]

⌇

WE NEVER WANT to mix up observation and evaluation. We don't want to trick ourselves into thinking it's what the other person does that's the cause of our anger. It's the stimulus. [19]

⌇

SO WHAT WE want to do as we use NVC to manage anger is to go more deeply into it, to see what is going on within us when we are angry, to be able to get at the need—which is the root of anger—and then fulfill that need. For teaching purposes, I sometimes refer to anger as similar to the warning light on the dashboard of a car—it's giving you useful information about what the engine needs. You wouldn't want to hide or disconnect or ignore it. You'd want to slow down the car and figure out what the light's trying to tell you. [9]

⮾

THE FIRST THING to do when we start to get angry or defensive is to recognize that we didn't hear the other person. What breaks us out of these fights is our consciousness. If we hear anything but a gift in the other person's message, we didn't hear them. You have to notice when your NVC ears have fallen off. Anger is a wonderful clue; it's like a wake-up call to an NVC-er. As soon as I get angry or defensive or hear an attack or demand, I know that I didn't hear the other person. Instead of connecting to what's going on in them, I'm up in my head judging that they're wrong in some way. If I'm using NVC, I know to shut up as quickly as possible, put my NVC ears on, and listen to myself. I've wounded myself if I have judging ears. How do I do this?

I listen to myself. I give myself empathy. I see how much pain I've created for myself by putting on my judging ears and hearing all of that. I notice that this has happened and then I shut up and enjoy the show going on in my head. It's just like watching a movie. [1]

⮾

THE FIRST STEP in expressing our anger, managing it in harmony with NVC, is to identify the stimulus for our anger without confusing it with our evaluation. The second step is to be conscious that it is our evaluation of people—in the form of judgments that imply wrongness—that causes our anger. [9]

⮾

THE THIRD STEP involves looking for the need that is the root of our anger. This is built on the assumption that we get angry because our needs are not getting met. The problem is that we're not in touch with our needs. Instead of being directly connected to our need, we go up to our head and start thinking of what's wrong with other people for not meeting our needs. The judgments we make of other people— which are the cause of our anger—are really *alienated expressions of unmet needs.* [9]

〜

I HAVE OUTLINED three steps in managing our anger using NVC:
1. Identify the stimulus for our anger, without confusing it with the evaluation.
2. Identify the internal image or judgment that is making us angry.
3. Transform this judgmental image into the need that it is expressing; in other words, bring our full attention to the need that is behind the judgment.

These three steps are done internally—we're not saying anything out loud. We're simply becoming aware that our anger is not caused by what the other person has done, but by our judgment, and then we are looking for the need behind the judgment. [9]

〜

THE FOURTH STEP includes saying to the other person four pieces of information. First, we reveal to them the stimulus: what they have done that is in conflict with our needs being fulfilled. Secondly, we express how we are feeling. Notice we are not repressing the anger. The anger has been transformed into a feeling such as sad, hurt, scared, frustrated, or the like. And then we follow up our expression of our feelings with the needs of ours that are not being fulfilled.

And now we add to those three pieces of information *a clear, present request of what we want from the other person* in relationship to our feelings and unmet needs. [9]

〜

AN EXERCISE I'D recommend is to list the kind of judgments that are likely to go on inside of you when you are angry. You might want to think of the most recent time that you have gotten angry, and ask yourself and write down what you were telling yourself that was making you angry.

When you have made an inventory of the kind of things you tell yourself in different situations that make you angry, you might then go back over this list and ask yourself, "What was I needing that was being expressed through that judgment?" And the more time we spend making these translations from judgments into needs, the more it will help us follow these procedures for expressing anger more quickly in real-life situations. [9]

Expressing Anger

NVC IS REALLY a way of fully expressing the anger. [9]

❧

THE FIRST STEP to fully expressing anger in NVC is to divorce the other person from any responsibility for our anger. We rid ourselves of thoughts such as, "He (or she or they) made me angry when they did that." Such thinking leads us to express our anger superficially by blaming or punishing the other person. . . . We are never angry because of what someone else did. We can identify the other person's behavior as the stimulus, but it is important to establish a clear separation between stimulus and cause. [5]

❧

TO FULLY EXPRESS anger requires full consciousness of our need. In addition, energy is required to get the need met. Anger, however, co-opts our energy by directing it toward punishing people rather than meeting our needs. [5]

❧

THE FOUR STEPS to expressing anger are (1) stop and breathe, (2) identify our judgmental thoughts, (3) connect with our needs, and (4) express our feelings and unmet needs. [5]

‿つ

TO ME, ANY kind of . . . blaming of other people, punishing, or hurting other people is a very superficial expression of our anger. We want something much more powerful than killing or hurting people physically or mentally. That's too weak. We want something much more powerful than that to fully express ourselves. [9]

Repressing Anger

IF YOU ARE angry, don't think you shouldn't be angry. Don't think there's anything wrong with being angry. That just creates more of a problem. Use the anger as a wake-up call that reminds you of two things: (1) A need of mine isn't getting met. (2) I'm thinking in a way almost guaranteed not to get it met, or to get it met in a way I'm going to pay for. [19]

‿つ

THE WORST THING we can do is repress the anger. Did you ever see the quotes of neighbors of serial killers? How they describe the serial killer? "What a nice person, never got angry." So the worst thing we can do for anger is to think that nice people don't get angry, and push it down. I'm not saying that. I'm saying anger is a helpful sign that our needs aren't getting met and we're thinking in a way that's creating violence on the planet, and is likely not to get our needs met for reasons we want them to get met. [19]

‿つ

WHEN IT COMES to managing anger, NVC shows us how to use anger as an alarm that tells us we are thinking in ways that are not likely to get our needs met, and are more likely to get us involved in interactions that

> "The four steps to expressing anger are (1) stop and breathe, (2) identify our judgmental thoughts, (3) connect with our needs, and (4) express our feelings and unmet needs.[5]

are not going to be very constructive for anyone. Our training stresses that *it is dangerous to think of anger as something to be repressed, or as something bad.*[9]

〜

THERE'S AN ENORMOUS amount of violence in me conditioned by cultural factors and other things. So, I enjoy that. I just sit back when I get that angry and I just watch this violent show going on in my head. I hear all these violent things I'd like to say, and I see these things I'd like to do to this person and then I listen to the pain that's behind it. And when I get to the pain behind it, there's always a release.

Then I can put my attention on the other person's humanness. I'm not repressing anything, quite the opposite. I'm enjoying it, this show going on, this violent show going in my head. . . .

I'm just not acting on it because to act on it is too superficial. If I jump in and blame this person, we're never going to get down to the pain behind all this. I'm not going to really be able to fully express my needs to this person and have them get it. We'll just get into a fight, and I know how that ends: even when I win, I don't feel good.[9]

〜

DON'T REPRESS YOUR anger, ever—don't push it down. Use it as a stimulus to come back to life. Be conscious when you're angry that you're not connected to your needs. You're up in your head playing a game we've been taught to play, called "Punitive God."[26]

〜

AGAIN, IF I connect to the other person's needs, I will never feel angry. I won't be *repressing* my anger, I simply won't feel it. I'm suggesting that how we feel is a result each moment of which of these four options we choose: Do we choose to go up to our head and judge the other person? Do we choose to go up to our head and judge our self? Do we choose to connect empathically with the other person's needs? Or do we choose to connect empathically with our needs?

It is that choice that determines our feelings. That's why Nonviolent Communication requires a very important word come after the word *because*—the word *I*, not the word *you*. For instance, "I feel angry because *I* ___." This reminds us that what we feel is not because of what the other person did, but the choice I made. [9]

ANGER SOUND BITES

- There's not a thing another person can do that can make us angry.

- Any thinking that is in your head that involves the word *should* is violence provoking.

- I don't think we get angry because our needs aren't getting met. I think we get angry because we have judgments about others.

- Anger is a natural feeling created by unnatural thinking.

- I'm not saying that it is wrong to judge people. . . . What's important is to be conscious that it's that judgment that makes us angry.

- Even if you don't say judgments out loud, your eyes show this kind of thinking.

- Use the words *I feel because I* . . . to remind us that what we feel is not because of what the other person did, but because of the choice I made.

- To me the life that's going on within us can be most clearly grasped by looking at what our needs are. Ask yourself, "What are my needs in this situation?"

- When I am connected to my needs I have strong feelings, but never anger. I see all anger as a result of life-alienated, violent, provocative thinking.

- Sadness is a feeling that mobilizes us to get our needs met. Anger is a feeling that mobilizes us to blame and punish others.

- To fully express the anger means getting our full consciousness on the need that isn't getting met.

- The best way I can get understanding from another person . . . is to give this person the understanding too. If I want them to hear my needs and feelings, I first need to empathize.

- When I give people the empathy they need, I haven't found it is that hard to get them to hear me.

- Anger is a very valuable feeling in NVC. It's a wake-up call. It tells us that I'm thinking in ways almost guaranteed not to meet my needs. Why? Because my energy is not connected to my needs, and I'm not even aware of what my needs are when I'm angry.[9]

PART IV

NVC IN RELATIONSHIPS

It may be most difficult
to empathize with those
we are closest to.[34]

9

BEING IN RELATIONSHIP

RELATIONSHIPS

IT MAY BE most difficult to empathize with those we are closest to. [34]

↪

BLAMING IS EASY. People are used to hearing blame; sometimes they agree with it and hate themselves—which doesn't stop them from behaving the same way—and sometimes they hate us for calling them racists or whatever—which also doesn't stop their behavior. [5]

↪

PLANS TO EXACT retribution are never going to make us safer. [34]

↪

PEOPLE DO NOT hear our pain when they believe they are at fault. [34]

↪

I'M SUGGESTING THAT if you want to be heard, you have a much better chance if you begin by connecting with what's alive in the other person. Show them that you don't see there's anything wrong with them for what they're saying. If you can communicate that message first, then I think you have a much better chance of being understood. [28]

↜

ASK BEFORE OFFERING advice or reassurance. [34]

↜

WHEN IT COMES to giving advice, never do so unless you've first received a request in writing, signed by a lawyer. [34]

↜

UPSET? ASK YOURSELF what this person does that is a trigger for judging them. [34]

↜

IT IS MY belief that all such analyses of other human beings are tragic expressions of our own values and needs. [5]

↜

BEHIND INTIMIDATING MESSAGES are simply people appealing to us to meet their needs. [34]

↜

A DIFFICULT MESSAGE to hear is an opportunity to enrich someone's life. [34]

↜

ALWAYS LISTEN TO what people need rather than what they are thinking about us. [34]

I SUGGEST THAT you never, never, never listen to what other people think about you. I predict you'll live longer and enjoy life more if you never hear what people think about you. And never take it personally. [8]

∿

WHEN SOMEBODY'S TELLING you what's wrong with you, the truth is [that] they have a need that isn't getting met. Hear that they're in pain. Don't hear the analysis. [34]

∿

WHEN YOU SAY something and don't say what you want back from others, you create more pain in relationships than you are probably conscious of. Other people have to guess, "Does she want me to say something cute and superficial about this thing, or is she really trying to tell me something else?" [1]

∿

UNDERSTANDING THE OTHER person's needs does not mean you have to give up your own needs. It does mean demonstrating to the other person that you are interested in *both* your needs and theirs. When they trust that, there's much more likelihood of everyone's needs getting met. [11]

∿

SEE, WOMEN HAVE been taught that once you see the other person's need, now you have to give up yours. So it's very costly to empathize, because once you empathize, then you're lost. How can you possibly stay connected to your needs, now that you see how much it means to this person? So then you can't see it as a mitzvah [awareness of the blessing of an opportunity to be of service]; it's a big pressure. [16]

∿

IT'S BEAUTIFUL TO care for others, but we have to be sure we don't lose our self in the process. [19]

~

HOW DO I meet both my own need to be nurturing, but to myself as well as the other? Stop and make sure you never agree to do what the other person wants unless it's play. [16]

~

IT'S NOT YOU that is the problem, it's that their needs aren't getting met. That's the problem. [22]

~

WHEN YOU'RE HEARING what another person says as meaning you did something wrong, that's a further violation of the other person because then, not only are they not getting the understanding that they need, now they get the feeling that their honesty creates problems for you. It's going to be harder for her to be honest in the future if she tries to tell what's going on with her and you think that you did something wrong. [1]

~

I WOULDN'T EXPECT someone who's been injured to hear my side until they felt that I had fully understood the depth of their pain. [34]

~

I STRONGLY RECOMMEND that whenever you're talking to somebody who is in pain, in relationship to you, before you come back to yourself and express what you feel, count to a million slowly. But if you're not good at math, then the other option is the one I use. "Is there more you want to say?" In other words, make sure when somebody starts to express pain to you, that before you shift the focus away from them onto you, they're finished. They've gotten all the empathy they want. [19]

A GIRAFFE NEVER tries to fix the other person's pain without a six-hour delay that gives the other person all the time they need to have their pain fully understood before you try to fix it. [22]

↩

WHEN WE ARE fully present to another person, there is an extraordinarily beautiful energy that works through human beings that can fix anything. But when we . . . think it's our responsibility to fix it, we block that energy. [30]

↩

WHENEVER I HAVE a close relationship with someone, one of the first things I want to get clear [is] please don't ever do anything for me. How will you know that you're doing it for me? You will feel some tinge of guilt, fear, anxiety, or resentment. Please only respond to my needs if it's meeting your needs. Now, for a yes-saying jackal, that'll blow their mind. This goes so much against their concept of love—to deny themselves and do for others. [13]

↩

GIRAFFES NEVER DO anything for other people. Giraffes live by the philosophy "me first and only." I feel really safe to say what I need from such people. If I say, "I'd like you to do this," if this is a person that lives by me-first-and-only, I know that if they do it, they're doing it for themselves, because they enjoy giving to me. I'm not going to get a bill for it later. But I've had so many of those yes-saying jackals and gotten bills for it later, you see. "After all I've done for you." [13]

↩

ANYTIME SOMEBODY DOES what we ask out of guilt, shame, duty, obligation, fear of punishment, anything that people do for us out of that energy, we're going to pay for it. We want people to do for us only when they're connected to that kind of a divine energy that exists in all of us. Divine energy is manifest to me by the joy we feel in giving to one another. [6]

⤳

WE NEED TO be able to make those explicit requests, especially when our need for love isn't getting met. Then we need to really be clear, what do I want this person to do to meet my need for love? If we can't answer that question, don't expect to get your need for love met. But many of us have been educated in the jackal school of love. That goes like this: "But if you really love me, you would know what I want without my having to tell you!" [19]

⤳

I BELIEVE IT is critical to be aware of the importance of people's reasons for behaving as we request. [5]

⤳

DON'T EVER EXPECT honesty until the person knows you have giraffe ears. [26]

⤳

I THINK THE need to enrich life is one of the most basic and powerful needs we all have. Now another way to say this is that we need to act from the divine energy within us. And I think that when we "are" that divine energy that there is nothing we like more—nothing in which we find more joy—than enriching life, than using our immense power to enrich life.

But whenever we are trying to meet this need of ours to "live" this divine energy, trying to contribute to life, there is also another need, and a request that goes with it. We have a need for information, and so we make a request for feedback from the person whose life we are trying to enrich. We want to know, "Is my intention being fulfilled by my action; was my attempt to contribute successful?"

In our culture that request gets distorted into our thinking that we have a "need" for the other person to love us for what we've done, to appreciate what we've done, to approve of us for what we've done. And that distorts and screws up the beauty of the whole process. It wasn't their approval that we needed. Our very intent was to use our energy to enrich life. But we need the feedback. How do I know my effort was successful unless I get feedback?

And I can use this feedback to help me know if I am coming out of divine energy. I know that I am coming out of divine energy when I am able to value a criticism as much as a thank you. [6]

$$\backsim$$

VITALITY DRAINS OUT of conversations when we lose connection with the feelings and needs generating the speaker's words, and with the requests associated with those needs. This effect is common when people talk without consciousness of what they are feeling, needing, or requesting. Instead of being engaged in an exchange of life energy with other human beings, we see ourselves becoming wastebaskets for their words.

How and when do we interrupt a dead conversation to bring it back to life? I'd suggest the best time to interrupt is when we've heard one word more than we want to hear. The longer we wait, the harder it is to be civil when we do step in. Our intention in interrupting is not to claim the floor for ourselves, but to help the speaker connect to the life energy behind the words being spoken. [5]

Autonomy

THIS OBJECTIVE OF getting what we want from other people, or getting them to do what we want them to do, threatens the autonomy of people, their right to choose what they want to do. And whenever people feel that they're not free to choose what they want to do, they are likely to resist, even if they see the purpose in what we are asking and would ordinarily want to do it. So strong is our need to protect our autonomy, that if we see that someone has this single-mindedness of purpose, if they are acting like they think that they know what's best for us and are not leaving it to us to make the choice of how we behave, it stimulates our resistance. [7]

⌒

AS LONG AS any human being of any age thinks you have single-mindedness of purpose, they'll probably resist. Or if they don't, and they do whatever you want, you'll probably pay for it. [10]

⌒

IF I SEE a person as being resistant, I think I've already lost the connection. So at those moments when people are speaking in a way that I used to call resistance . . . I hear it as a gift. This person, if I hear accurately, is teaching me what needs of theirs will have to be met before they can be comfortable with what I'm offering. [27]

⌒

WHAT I USED to call resistance, I now see as the person just telling me what their needs are that have to be addressed in order for us to connect. [27]

Please and Thank You

ALL THAT'S COMING at you ever from other people is please or thank you. That's the only two things that human beings are ever saying. Please and thank you. And both of them are precious messages if you hear them accurately. The thank you is a celebration of life; life has been made more wonderful. The please is an opportunity to make life more wonderful. [22]

" When we understand
the needs that motivate
our own and others' behavior,
we have no enemies. [34]

SEE, THERE'S ONLY two things that basically we ever really are saying as human beings, I believe. And that's please and thank you. So the language of giraffe is set up to make our please and thank you very clear, so that people do not hear anything that gets in the way of our giving to each other from the heart. [23]

ENEMY IMAGES

WHEN WE UNDERSTAND the needs that motivate our own and others' behavior, we have no enemies. [34]

↩

WE NEED TO liberate ourselves from enemy images, the thinking that says there is something wrong with the people who are part of these gangs. Now, that's not easy to do. It's hard to see that those who are doing these things are human beings like the rest of us. It's very challenging with gangs, and often it's just as difficult with individuals. [8]

↩

ONCE BOTH SIDES get over the enemy image and recognize each other's needs, it's amazing how the next part, which is looking for strategies to meet everyone's needs, becomes pretty easy by comparison. It's getting past the enemy images that's the hard work. It's getting people to see that you can't benefit at other people's expense. Once you have *that* clear, even complicated things like family squabbles aren't horrible to resolve because you've got people connecting at a human level.

The same thing applies to gangs. The most common elements I've found in the conflicts I've been asked to mediate are that people—instead of knowing how to say clearly what their needs and requests are—are quite eloquent in diagnosing other people's pathology: what's wrong with them for behaving as they do. Whether it's two individuals, two groups, or two countries that have conflicts, they begin the discussion with enemy images, telling the other person what's wrong with them. The divorce courts—and the bombs—are never far away.[8]

∽

ENEMY IMAGES ARE the main reason conflicts don't get resolved.[34]

MARRIAGE AND INTIMACY

IT'S HARDER TO relate in marriage than outside of it because of all the crazy things we're taught about what marriage means.[23]

∽

IF YOU WANT to have . . . what's originally very beautiful, turn into something ugly very quick, define marriage so that once you are married you have certain obligations and commitments. Commitments defined as demands. Now, that takes what otherwise could be done joyfully and turns it into something ugly.[20]

∽

AND THAT'S WHY marriage is a real challenge, because you see many people are taught that love and marriage mean denying yourself and doing for the other person.[23]

∽

I FIND I enjoy the person I'm living with much more if I don't think of her as "my wife," because in the culture I grew up in, when someone says "my wife," they start to think of her as some kind of property.[1]

∽

WHAT ARE YOU afraid to tell me? And what could I do to make life more wonderful for you? And what have I done that's made life more wonderful for you? If you answer those three questions, you can get more connection than many people get in a lifetime of being intimate. [12]

~

SO THAT'S ONE of the most frequent things that gets in the way of intimate relationships—asking for something that isn't doable. [20]

~

MEN THROUGHOUT THE planet—and there are exceptions to this—come from the John Wayne school of expressing emotions, the Clint Eastwood, the Rambo school, where you kind of grunt. And instead of saying clearly what's going on inside of you, you label people as John Wayne would when he walked into a tavern in the movies. He never, even if there were guns trained on him, said, "I'm scared." He might have been out in the desert for six months, but he never said, "I'm lonely." But how did John communicate? John communicated by labeling people. It's a simple classification system. They were either a good guy—buy them a drink—or a bad guy—kill them.

With that way of communicating, which was how I was trained to communicate basically, you don't learn how to get in touch with your own emotions. If you're being trained to be a warrior, you want to keep your feelings out of your consciousness. Well, to be married to a warrior is not a very rich experience for a woman who may have been playing dolls while the men were out playing war. She wants intimacy, but the man doesn't have a vocabulary that makes it easy to do that.

On the other hand, women are not taught to be very clear about their needs. They've been taught for several centuries to deny their own needs and take care of others. So they often depend on the man for leadership and expect him to kind of guess what she needs and wants and to fulfill that, to take care of that. So I see these issues regularly, but as I say, there are certainly a lot of individual differences. [1]

IF YOU EVEN have a concept of rejection in your consciousness, it's going to make intimacy very difficult. So one of, for me, the most important parts of an intimate relationship is to receive a *no* as a memnoon [a request that blesses the one who is asked], as a mitzvah [the blessing of an opportunity to be of service]. The person is giving me an opportunity to meet a need of theirs. A *no* is always a tragic expression of a need—tragic if the other person has jackal ears on and they hear it as a rejection. If we have giraffe ears on, it's a gift. That person is telling us what need of theirs they're trying to meet that keeps them from meeting our need. Then it's a memnoon. [20]

~

YOU HAVE TO have a built-in detector in your relationship, so that before you allow a person to meet any of your needs, they have to pass this test: that what they're doing is motivated only out of memnoon energy [the energy of a request that blesses the one who is asked]. There isn't a trace of motivation in them doing it because they're afraid they'll be punished if they don't, hoping that you will love them more if they do—a reward, in other words. No guilt. No shame. No concept of duty or obligation. [20]

LOVE

IT MAY HELP you to understand that Nonviolent Communication really grew from my attempt to understand the concept of love and how to manifest it, how to *do* it. I had come to the conclusion that love is not just something we feel, but it is something we manifest, something we do, something we have. And love is something we give: We give of ourselves in particular ways. It's a gift when you reveal yourself nakedly and honestly, at any given moment, for no other purpose than to reveal what's alive in you. Not to blame, criticize, or punish. Just "Here I am, and here is what I would like. This is my vulnerability at this moment." To me, that giving is a manifestation of love.

Another way we give of ourselves is through how we receive another person's message. It's a gift to receive it empathically, connecting with what's alive in them, making no judgment. It's a gift when we try to hear what is alive in the other person and what they would like. So Nonviolent Communication is just a manifestation of what I understand love to be. In that way it's similar to the Judeo-Christian concepts of "Love your neighbor as yourself" and "Judge not lest you be judged." [1]

ᔕ

WHAT I'M SHARING with you today is really what I've learned about love—how to live it. It's something you live, not something you feel. So I would say that we manifest love to the degree to which we openly reveal ourselves without criticizing others. And then the other half is how we respond to other peoples' messages to us. So I would say love is how we reveal ourselves, and how we receive other peoples' messages. That's the most powerful way I know of meeting needs for love. [10]

ᔕ

LOVE IS NOT denying ourselves and doing for others. But rather, love is honestly expressing whatever our feelings and needs are and empathetically receiving the other person's feelings and needs. [23]

ᔕ

LOVE IS A very precious need. It's a need, a central need of human beings. [20]

ᔕ

LOVE, FOR ME, is a need. That's quite different from a jackal definition of love. Jackals define love as a feeling. So this creates great pain when jackals and giraffes get together, unless the giraffe really knows how to handle the violent question, "Do you love me?" "Jackal, when you ask do I love you, are you using the word *love* as a feeling? Do you mean do I feel warm, tender, cuddly emotions toward you?" "Yes!" "I just needed to check this out, Jackal. Because, see, we giraffes do not use the word *love* as a feeling. We use it as a need. But since I know you use it as a feeling, now, and I can see how important it is to you, I will do my best to answer you honestly. So please ask the question again." "Do you love me?" "When?" [*laughter*] "When?!" "Jackal, if you use it as a feeling, feelings change every few seconds. How can I possibly answer you honestly without reference to a specific time and place?" "Well—what about right now?" ". . . No." [*laughter*] "But try me again in a few minutes, you never know." [12]

ᔓ

IN THE CULTURE I grew up in, the way I was taught to define the actions to meet this need for love were pretty sickening. Just the music, if you listen to the music . . . "I ain't nothin' without you, baby." It was like love almost always meant not to be oneself. One was to be a slavish appendage to this other creature, dependent on this other person. Dependency all mixed up, a lot of scary stuff in it. So it took me a while to get clear what actions do I want from other people to meet my need for love. [20]

ᔓ

SO TO COMMUNICATE this quality of unconditional love, respect, acceptance to other people, this doesn't mean that we have to like what they're doing. It doesn't mean we have to be permissive and give up our needs or values. What it requires is that we show people the same quality of respect when they don't do what we ask, as when they do. After we have shown that quality of respect through empathy, through taking the time to understand why they didn't do what we would like, we can then pursue how we might influence them to willingly do what we ask. In some cases, where people are behaving in a serious way that threatens our needs or safety and there's not time or ability to communicate about it, we may even use force.

But unconditional love requires that no matter how people behave, they trust that they'll receive a certain quality of understanding from us.[7]

FOUR QUESTIONS

I'M GOING TO ask you four questions. If you are married or partnered, then pretend that you'll be speaking with your partner or spouse. If you want to focus on some other relationship, pick someone you're close to, perhaps a good friend. Now as your NVC partner, I'm going to ask you the four questions that deeply interest NVC-speaking people around all relationships, but particularly intimate ones. Please write down your answer to each of these four questions as though you were asked by this other person. Reader: We invite you to do this on your own on a separate sheet of paper.

The first question: Would you tell me one thing that I do as your partner or friend that makes life less than wonderful for you?

You see, as an NVC-er I don't want to take any action or say anything that doesn't enrich your life. So it would be a great service if, anytime I do something that isn't enriching your life, you bring that to my attention. Could you think of one thing that I do—or don't do—that makes life less than wonderful for you? Write down one thing.

Now the second question. As an NVC-speaking person, not only do I want to know what I do that makes life less than wonderful for you, it's also important for me to be able to connect with your feelings moment by moment. To be able to play the game of giving to one another from our hearts, your feelings are critical and I need to be aware of them. It's stimulating when we can be in touch with one another's feelings. My second question then:

When I do what I do, how do you feel?

Write down how you feel.

Let's move to the third question. As an NVC-speaking person, I realize that how we feel is a result of what our needs are and what is happening to our needs. When our needs are getting fulfilled, then we have feelings that fall under the heading of "pleasurable feelings," like happy, satisfied, joyful, blissful, content . . . and when our needs are not being satisfied, we have the kind of feelings that you just wrote down. So this is question three:

What needs of yours are not getting met?

I'd like you to tell me why you feel as you do in terms of your needs: "I feel as I do because I would have liked _____ (or because I was wanting, wishing, or hoping for _____)." Write down what you need in this format.

Now the NVC-er is excited because he wants to get on to this next question, which is the center of life for all NVC-speaking people. I can't wait to hear the answer to this. Everybody ready for the big NVC question?

I am aware that I am doing something that is not enriching your life and that you have certain feelings about that. You've told me what needs of yours are not getting fulfilled. Now, please tell me what I can do to make your most wonderful dreams come true. That is what NVC is all about:

What can we do to enrich one another's lives?

NVC is about clearly communicating those four things to other people at any given moment. Of course, the situation is not always about our needs getting met. We also say "thank you" in NVC and tell people how they have truly enriched our lives by telling them the first three things. We tell them (1) what they've done to enrich us, (2) what our feelings are, and (3) what needs of ours have been fulfilled by their actions. I believe that, as human beings, there are only two things that we are basically saying: "please" and "thank you." The language of NVC is set up to make our "please" and "thank you" very clear so that people do not hear anything that gets in the way of our giving to one another from the heart. [1]

HEARING AND SAYING NO

Hearing No

A *NO* IS always a need and a request, if we hear it accurately. [20]

‿

THE KEY TO fostering connection in the face of a *no* is always yes to something else and, as such, it is the beginning, not the end, of a conversation. Hear the *yes* behind the *no*. [34]

‿

IN OUR NONVIOLENT Communication training, we show people how to hear the human behind the *no*. To be conscious that, if we hear a *no*, we're hearing very little about what's really alive in this person at this moment. [32]

‿

IF WE HAVE giraffe ears, we know that a *no* is just as good a gift as a *yes*. [16]

‿

IF THE OTHER person says no, with these [giraffe] ears on, you can't hear no. With these ears on, you are conscious that a *no* is a poor expression of a *yes*. [21]

‿

EVERY *NO*, IF we hear it accurately, is a mitzvah [awareness of the blessing of an opportunity to be of service]. It's telling us what that person's need is. If we don't have giraffe ears—if we have jackal ears—we hear it as a rejection. Or we take it that our needs aren't valued, or our needs are a burden. [16]

UNTIL YOU HEAR the need behind the *no*, it's going to be hard to figure out a way for everybody's needs to get met. On the other hand, when everybody's needs are expressed and understood, the problem will solve itself. [20]

∽

EMPATHIZING WITH SOMEONE'S *no* protects us from taking it personally. [34]

Rejection

IT'S NEVER THE *no* that's the problem. It's what we tell ourselves when the person says no, that's the problem. If we tell ourselves that that's a rejection, then that's a problem, because rejection hurts. [23]

∽

BECAUSE OF OUR tendency to read rejection into someone else's *no* and *I don't want to . . .* , these are important messages for us to be able to empathize with. If we take them personally, we may feel hurt without understanding what's actually going on within the other person. When we shine the light of consciousness on the feelings and needs behind someone else's *no*, however, we become cognizant of what they are wanting that prevents them from responding as we would like. [5]

∽

NOW, AS SOON as I put on these [giraffe] ears, a miracle takes place: Rejection vanishes from the earth. I never hear a *no*. I never hear a *don't want*. Judgments and criticism vanish from the earth. Then all I hear is the truth, which to an NVC-speaking person is this: All that other people are ever expressing are their feelings and needs. The only things that people are ever saying, no matter how they are expressing it, are how they are and what they would like to make life even better. When a person says no, that's just a poor way of letting us know what they really want. We don't want to make it worse by hearing a rejection. We hear what they want. [1]

〜

YOU ONLY HAVE to worry about rejection if you think there is such a thing. We never have to worry about rejection if we have NVC ears on. There is no such thing. If you have NVC ears on, you never hear a *no*. It doesn't exist. You know that a *no* is a tragic expression of a need. So you hear the need behind the *no*. There's no such thing as rejection. You're hearing what need of the other person keeps them from saying yes—that's not a rejection. [3]

Saying No

TO SAY NO in giraffe we never use the following words—*no*. To say no in giraffe, never say no. Next, *I don't want to*. Never say, "I don't want to." Never say, "I'm not willing." Never say, "I can't." Never say, "I don't have time." . . . Never say, "It's not possible." [22]

〜

THE BIGGEST PART of saying no to somebody is to show an empathic connection with the need, which means they feel that their need was received as a gift. . . . You show an empathic connection for the other person's needs. You say your needs at the moment that you'd like to attend to, and then you end on a request that searches for a way to get everybody's needs met. [12]

〜

HOW DO WE say no in giraffe? Well, the first step is probably the hardest and that is to show sincerely in our eyes that we received a beautiful gift from this request. When people trust that their request is received as a gift then no matter how else we say no, it's going to be easier for them to hear. What's painful for people is not hearing no, it's feeling like their need doesn't matter. [22]

10

HEALING AND RECONCILIATION

WE DON'T WANT to depend on the other person's availability for our own healing to take place. Especially if they're not alive anymore, if they're inaccessible. Fortunately we can heal *fully* without the other person being involved. [2]

↵

THE FIRST STAGE in the healing process is to get someone the empathy they need. There are three ways to do it: You can give it as a third party, you can play the role of the other person involved, or get that other person there to give it in person. [2]

↵

PEOPLE WHO HAVE been in a lot of pain tell me that they've had somebody say: "You should empathize with the other person. If you empathize you'll feel better about it." It's true I think that the healing is deep when we can empathize with what's going on in the person who raped us, who did something harmful to us. But to ask people to do that before they have had the empathy they need first is just to commit further violence to them. [2]

SO GETTING EMPATHY for the person who did the act that stimulated the other person's pain, it's very important that that be done when the person in pain is ready to empathize. [18]

∽

I WORK WITH a lot of people who have been in stress. And almost as soon as they have the empathy they need, they scream, when I'm playing the role of the other person, "How could you have done it?" There's a hunger to empathize with the other person. After we've had the empathy ourselves. But to try to go there too early is just to make things worse. [19]

∽

IN SITUATIONS OF pain, I recommend first getting the empathy necessary to go beyond the thoughts occupying our heads and recognize our deeper needs. [5]

∽

EMPATHY IS THE most powerful part of healing. [19]

∽

PEOPLE HEAL FROM their pain when they have an authentic connection with another human being. [34]

∽

TIME AND AGAIN, people transcend the paralyzing effects of psychological pain when they have sufficient contact with someone who can hear them empathically. [34]

∽

I'VE FOUND OUT that the empathy is extremely powerful and it can be given in three ways. One, I could have given her the empathy as

> "People heal from their pain
> when they have an authentic
> connection with another
> human being. [26]

myself, as Marshall. But I have seen in just experimenting [that] it's more powerful if I give it playing the role of the other person. And it's even more powerful if I have the other person here and pull the other person by the ears and help them to give the empathy themselves. [19]

~

GETTING IN TOUCH with unmet needs is important to the healing process. [34]

~

I SOMETIMES WORK with people who have been raped or tortured and where the perpetrator is absent, I would assume their role. Oftentimes the victim is surprised to hear me in the role-play saying the same thing they had heard from their perpetrator, and press me with the question, "But how did you know?" I believe the answer to that question is that I know because I am that person. And so are we all. [5]

PAST VS NOW

THE MORE WE talk about the past, the less we heal from it. [2]

~

WHAT NEEDS TO be understood is not the details of the past. Our creativity is in nakedly revealing what's still alive in us at this moment in relationship to the past. [30]

~

WE CAN'T CHANGE the past. But we can do something to make things better now. But the more we talk about the past, the less likely we are to get what we want now. [26]

~

THE FIRST STAGE of healing involves empathizing with what's alive right now in relationship to what happened. [2]

⤶

SO, THE FIRST step, if we want to heal or help somebody to heal, put the focus on what's alive now, not what happened in the past. If there is a discussion of the past, five words, no more. When you ran away from home; when you hit me, whatever. Okay. Enough of that. Now let's deal with what's alive in us now in relationship to that. [18]

⤶

THAT PAIN THAT'S still alive from all that happened in the past is kind of scary. You really have to go into it deeply, in order to get the empathy we need. It's sometimes much easier to keep telling the story. [30]

⤶

NOW WHAT WE need to do when we have all this information about the past is not to go there. We deal in Nonviolent Communication healing, with what's alive right now as the result of what happened in the past. So the more we know about what happened in the past, the harder it is to empathize because we get into intellectual understanding. And that doesn't create the empathic connection that healing requires. That's why the more we've studied psychology, like I did, the harder it is to empathize. [19]

⤶

IN MY TRAINING in psychoanalysis, I was trained to spend a lot of time with people exploring what happened in the past. And now in the last several years I find that we get further in twenty minutes talking about what's alive now than twenty months talking about what happened in the past. [19]

I HAVE FOUND that talking about what happened in the past not only doesn't help healing, it often perpetuates and increases pain. It's like reliving the pain. This goes very much against what I was taught in my training in psychoanalysis, but I've learned over the years that you heal by talking about what's going on in the moment, in the now.

Certainly it's stimulated by the past, and we don't deny how the past is affecting the present, but we don't "dwell" on it. [8]

⮑

MOST OF THE stories we tell get in the way of our getting what we want. Especially if we want understanding for our present pain and we think we have to tell our listener what happened in the past. By the time we get to the present pain, they're asleep. [22]

⮑

WE DON'T NEED to talk about what happened. We need to talk about what's alive in us right now about what happened. That's where the healing takes place. That's where the connection takes place. So the fewer words for the observation the better. The real focus of the message needs to be what's alive in us right now, our present feelings and needs. [22]

⮑

IT'S THE NOW where the healing takes place. [19]

⮑

I WOULD LIKE to explore what would happen if we could make movies or television shows of this process, because I've seen that when two people go through the process with other people watching, that vicarious learning, healing, and reconciliations happen. I would like to explore ways to use the media to get masses of people to go quickly through this process together. [6]

FORGIVENESS

WHEN THE FORGIVENESS is there, the reconciliation is the easy part. [30]

⊷

GIRAFFE FORGIVENESS IS empathy. When you empathize with somebody for why they did what they did, there's nothing to forgive. You only forgive when you think that what the other person did was wrong or bad. But if you empathize, you see that human beings, every moment, every human being, is doing the best they know how at that moment to meet their needs. [19]

⊷

FORGIVENESS IN A Nonviolent Communication way [is] a consciousness that every human being is doing what they're doing not because they're good boys and girls or evil boys and girls—it's the best they know to meet their needs at that moment. [19]

⊷

SO FORGIVENESS IS empathy. [30]

⊷

WHEN I USE the term *forgiveness*, I'm going to talk about this beautiful connection between people. It takes place when a certain quality of empathy has taken place between the parties. [30]

⊷

THE MORE YOU talk about the past, I will suggest, the more it gets in the way of reconciliation and forgiveness. [30]

NVC SELF-FORGIVENESS: connecting with the need we were trying to meet when we took the action that we now regret. [34]

11

CONFLICT RESOLUTION

RESPECT IS A key element of successful conflict resolution. [11]

〜

SPEAKING PEACE IS a way of connecting with others that allows our natural compassion to flourish. Around the world—from troubled families to dysfunctional bureaucracies to war-ravaged countries—I've found no more effective means of getting to a peaceful resolution of conflict. In fact, speaking peace using Nonviolent Communication offers the promise of reducing or even eliminating conflict in the first place. [8]

〜

MOST ATTEMPTS AT resolution search for compromise, which means everybody gives something up and neither side is satisfied. NVC is different; our objective is to meet everyone's needs fully. [5]

〜

MANY MEDIATIONS I have witnessed consist of waiting for people to wear down to the point where they'll accept any compromise. This is very different from a resolution in which everyone's needs are met and nobody experiences loss. [5]

↬

WE DO NOT look for compromise; rather, we seek to resolve the conflict to everyone's complete satisfaction. [34]

↬

TO PRACTICE THIS process of conflict resolution, we must completely abandon the goal of *getting people to do what we want.* [11]

↬

THE MORE WE empathize with the other party, the safer we feel. [34]

↬

IT HAS BEEN my experience that if we keep our focus on needs, our conflicts tend toward a mutually satisfactory resolution. Keeping our focus on needs, we express our own needs, clearly understand the needs of others, and avoid any language that implies wrongness of the other party. [11]

↬

OVER THE COURSE of several decades, I've used Nonviolent Communication to resolve conflicts around the world. I've met with unhappy couples, families, workers and their employers, and ethnic groups at war with each other. My experience has taught me that it's possible to resolve just about any conflict to everybody's satisfaction. All it takes is a lot of patience, the willingness to establish a human connection, the intention to follow NVC principles until you reach a resolution, and trust that the process will work. [5]

↬

IN NVC-STYLE CONFLICT resolution, creating a connection between the people who are in conflict is the most important thing. This is what enables all the other steps of NVC to work, because it's not until you have forged that connection that each side will seek to know exactly what the other side is feeling and needing. The parties also need to know from the start that the objective is *not* to get the other side to do what they want them to do. And once the two sides understand that, it becomes possible—sometimes even easy—to have a conversation about how to meet their needs. [5]

෴

WHEN TWO DISPUTING parties have each had an opportunity to fully express what they are observing, feeling, needing, and requesting—and each has empathized with the other—a resolution can usually be reached that meets the needs of both sides. At the very least, the two can agree, in goodwill, to disagree. [5]

෴

WHEN I AM called into a conflict resolution, I begin by guiding the participants to a caring and respectful quality of connection among themselves. Only after this connection is present do I engage them in a search for strategies to resolve the conflict. At that time we do not look for *compromise*; rather, we seek to resolve the conflict to everyone's complete satisfaction. To practice this process of conflict resolution, we must completely abandon the goal of *getting people to do what we want.* Instead, we focus on creating the conditions whereby *everyone's needs will be met.* [11]

෴

WHEN WE CAN connect at the need level, when we see one another's humanness, it's amazing how conflicts which seem unsolvable become solvable. I do a lot of work with people in conflict. Husbands and wives, parents and children, tribes of people. Many of these people think they have a conflict which can't be resolved. And it's been amazing to me over the years that I've been doing conflict resolution and mediation work, what happens when you can get people over their diagnosis of one another, get them connected at the need level to what's going on in one another, how conflicts which seem impossible to resolve seem like they almost resolve themselves. [6]

↬

UNFORTUNATELY, I'VE FOUND that very few people are literate in expressing needs. Instead they have been trained to criticize, insult, and otherwise communicate in ways that create distance among people. As a result, even in conflicts for which resolutions exist, resolutions are not found. And instead of both parties expressing their own needs and understanding the needs of the other party, both sides play the game of who's right? That game is more likely to end in various forms of verbal, psychological, or physical violence than in peaceful resolution of differences. [11]

↬

MANY OF US have great difficulty expressing our needs: we have been taught by society to criticize, insult, and otherwise (mis)communicate in ways that keep us apart. In a conflict, both parties usually spend too much time intent on proving themselves right, and the other party wrong, rather than paying attention to their own and the other's needs. And such verbal conflicts can far too easily escalate into violence—and even war. [5]

↬

AT THE POINT where either party hears themselves criticized, diagnosed, or intellectually interpreted, I predict their energy will turn toward self-defense and counter-accusations rather than toward resolutions that meet everyone's needs. [11]

THE MORE EXPERIENCE I have gained in mediating conflicts over the years and the more I've seen what leads families to argue and nations to go to war, the more convinced I am that most schoolchildren could solve these conflicts. If we could just say, "Here are the needs of both sides. Here are the resources. What can be done to meet these needs?" conflicts would be easily resolved. But instead, our thinking is focused on dehumanizing one another with labels and judgments until even the simplest of conflicts becomes very difficult to solve. NVC helps us avoid that trap, thereby enhancing the chances of reaching a satisfying resolution. [5]

⤳

THIS ABILITY TO sense what people need is crucial in mediating conflicts. We can help by sensing what both sides need, put it into words, and then we help each side hear the other side's needs. This creates a quality of connection that moves the conflict to successful resolution. [11]

⤳

IT'S IMPORTANT TO avoid moving hastily into strategies, as this may result in a compromise that lacks the deep quality of authentic resolution that is possible. By fully hearing each other's needs before addressing solutions, parties in conflict are much more likely to adhere to the agreements they make. . . . The process of resolving conflict has to end with actions that meet everybody's needs. It is the presentation of strategies in clear, present, positive action language that moves conflicts toward resolution. [5]

⤳

AFTER WE HAVE helped parties in a conflict express their needs and connect with the needs of others, then I suggest we move on to look for strategies that meet everyone's needs. In my experience, if we move too quickly to strategies, we may find some compromises, but we won't have the same quality of resolution. If we thoroughly understand needs before moving to proposed solutions, we increase the likelihood that both parties will stay with the agreement.

Of course, it's not enough just to help each side see what the other side needs. We must end with action, action that meets everyone's needs. This requires that we be able to express proposed strategies clearly in present, positive, action language. [11]

⮑

THE MORE WE can be clear what response we're wanting *right now*, the more quickly conflict moves toward resolution. [11]

⮑

IT'S VERY IMPORTANT, in expressing our requests, to be respectful of the other person's reaction regardless of whether they agree to the request. One of the most important messages another person can give us is "no" or "I don't want to." If we listen well to this message, it helps us understand the other person's needs. If we are listening to other peoples' needs, we will see that every time a person says no, they're really saying they have a need that is not addressed by our strategy, which keeps them from saying yes. If we can teach ourselves to hear the need behind that *no*, we will find an openness toward getting everyone's needs met.

Of course, if we hear the *no* as a rejection, or if we start to blame the other person for saying no, then it's not likely that we're going to find a way of getting everyone's needs met. It's key that, throughout the process, we keep everyone's attention focused on *meeting everyone's needs.*

I'm very optimistic about what happens in any conflict if we create this quality of connection. If all sides in a conflict get clear about what they need and hear the other side's needs, if people express their strategies in clear action language, then even if the other person says no, the focus returns to meeting *needs*. If we all do this, we will easily find strategies that get everyone's needs met. [11]

CONFLICTS, EVEN OF long-standing duration, can be resolved if we can just keep the flow of communication going in which people come out of their heads and stop criticizing and analyzing each other, and instead get in touch with their needs, and hear the needs of others, and realize the interdependence that we all have in relation to each other. We can't win at somebody else's expense. We can only fully be satisfied when the other person's needs are fulfilled as well as our own. [34]

∽

MAKE YOUR GOAL to attend to your underlying needs and to aim for a resolution so satisfying that everyone involved has their needs met also. [34]

∽

THE MOST POWERFUL thing we can do to begin a dialog with a person with whom we have a conflict is to communicate with them in a way in which they feel absolutely no criticism for what they're doing. Our goal is to create a quality of connection (empathic connection) that allows everyone's needs to be met. We listen using Nonviolent Communication to hear what the person feels and needs. We tune in to the message being communicated through their verbal and nonverbal communication. With Nonviolent Communication, we hear every message as an expression of a feeling and a need. Nonviolent Communication also requires being conscious of the difference between the *protective* use of force and the *punitive* use of force. We need to be clear that whatever we say is not intended to punish—that our intention is to protect. Instead of denying the other person's choice, we say what choice we will exercise. We express our needs in the form of clear, present requests. Praise, compliments, and expressions of gratitude are often heard as judgments. To create the quality of connection that is our goal, it's just as important that people hear our appreciation as our messages of distress. It's often helpful to check with the other person to make sure the message given was the one received. And finally, even more than your words, your presence is the most precious gift you can give to another human being. [10]

12

PARENTING

I OFTEN TELL the parents that I'm working with that hell is having children and thinking there's such a thing as a good parent.[7]

⬭

I OFFER YOU that reassuring advice given to me by my daughter, that nobody's perfect, to remember that anything that's worth doing is worth doing poorly. And the job of parenting, of course, is extremely worth doing, but we're going to do it poorly at times. If we're going to be brutal with ourselves when we're not perfect parents, our children are going to suffer for that.[7]

⬭

IF EVERY TIME we're less than perfect, we're going to blame ourselves and attack ourselves, our children are not going to benefit from that. So the goal I would suggest is not to be perfect parents, it's to become progressively less stupid parents—by learning from each time that we're not able to give our children the quality of understanding that they need, that we're not able to express ourselves honestly. In my experience, each of these times usually means that we're not getting the emotional support we need as parents, in order to give our children what they need.[7]

〜

WHEN I WAS a jackal parent, I was all confused about some central concepts. Like I confused respect for authority with fear of authority. I confused discipline, self-discipline, with obedience. I kept saying I wanted to teach my children self-discipline, but I was getting it mixed up with obedience.[23]

〜

HAVING BEEN EDUCATED, as I was, to think about parenting, I thought that it was the job of a parent to make children behave. You see, once you define yourself as an authority, a teacher or parent, in the culture that I was educated in, you then see it as your responsibility to make people that you label a "child" or a "student" behave in a certain way.

I now see what a self-defeating objective this is, because I have learned that anytime it's our objective to get another person to behave in a certain way, people are likely to resist no matter what it is we're asking for. This seems to be true whether the other person is two or ninety-two years of age.[7]

〜

I'LL BE FOREVER grateful to my children for educating me about the limitations of the objective of getting other people to do what you want. They taught me that, first of all, I couldn't make them do what I want. I couldn't make them do anything. I couldn't make them put a toy back in the toy box. I couldn't make them make their bed. I couldn't make them eat. Now, that was quite a humbling lesson for me as a parent, to learn about my powerlessness, because somewhere I had gotten it into my mind that it was the job of a parent to make a child behave. And here were these young children teaching me this humbling lesson, that I couldn't make them do anything. All I could do is make them wish they had.

And whenever I would be foolish enough to do that, that is, to make them wish they had, they taught me a second lesson about parenting and power that has proven very valuable to me over the years. And that lesson was that anytime I would make them wish they had, they would make me wish I hadn't made them wish they had. Violence begets violence. [7]

⮑

SEE, THAT'S WHAT you have to get across, unconditional love. Not that you are loved more when you do help than when you don't. Not that you are loved more when you brush your teeth than when you don't. You have a certain quality of connection that's there, separate from whether you live up to my standards. Unconditional love. [13]

⮑

WE NEED TO be able to tell children whether what they're doing is in harmony with our needs, or in conflict with our needs, but to do it in a way that doesn't stimulate guilt or shame on the child's part. [7]

⮑

PEOPLE CAN OFTEN mistake what I'm talking about as permissiveness or not giving children the direction they need, instead of understanding that it's a different quality of direction. It's a direction that comes from two parties trusting each other, rather than one party forcing his or her authority on another. [7]

⮑

I'VE WORKED IN some cultures where I see three- and four-year-olds doing the work of many adults. Really well. Because they really see how they're contributing to the family. They really see what the family needs them to do. Now you go to the middle classes in the United States, where you ask the parents, "Why do you want the child to do it?" "Well, they have to learn some responsibility." But it's a kind of a made-up thing . . . they're trying to give tasks, but it doesn't have the same kind of meaning to the child. Or where guilt-inducement is used to try to get them to do it. . . . You can have a child who has no work to do resist it, see, compared to three- and four-year-olds who are doing twice as much work in another culture and enjoying it. But it all has to do with how we present it to them. [13]

⤶

FEAR OF CORPORAL punishment obscures children's awareness of the compassion underlying the parent's demands. [34]

⤶

IN THE PUNITIVE use of force, the person using such force has made a moralistic judgment of the other person, a judgment that implies some kind of wrongness that is deserving of punishment. This person deserves to suffer for what they've done. That's the whole idea of punishment. It comes out of these ideas that human beings are basically sinful, evil creatures and the corrective process is to make them penitent. We have to get them to see how terrible they are for doing what they're doing. And the way we make them penitent is to use some form of punishment to make them suffer. Sometimes this can be a physical punishment in the form of spanking, or it could be a psychological punishment in the form of trying to make them hate themselves, through making them feel guilty or ashamed.

The thinking behind the protective use of force is radically different. There is no consciousness that the other person is bad or deserving of punishment. Our consciousness is fully focused on our needs. We are conscious of what need of ours is in danger. But we are not in any way implying badness or wrongness to the child. [7]

⤶

HOW DO WE get children to stop lying? And I have an easy answer, but the parents never like it. I say stop blaming and punishing. You have no lying then. Lying is adaptive in a punitive structure. You're a fool to tell the truth in a punitive structure. [22]

❧

ONE OF THE things that I find very important to prepare our children with is to show them how to maintain their own integrity, their own value system, even if they are going to be in structures that have different values than they have. [31]

❧

I WAS VERY good with my children under these conditions: I'd have an hour of empathy before I talked with them, talk to them for five minutes and then another hour of empathy, go back for another five minutes. And I'm exaggerating for some humor, but really for me to parent the way that I wanted to, I needed a supportive community around me. Because that is an important job, and what job do we want to do better than that? [18]

❧

WE CAN ONLY really give in a loving way to the degree that we are receiving similar love and understanding. So that's why I strongly recommend that we look at how we might create a supportive community for ourselves among our friends and others, who can give us the understanding we need to be present to our children in a way that will be good for them and good for us. [7]

❧

I WOULD RATHER take my time and come from an energy that I choose in communicating with my children, rather than habitually responding in a way that I have been trained to do, when it's not really in harmony with my own values. Sadly, we will often get much more reinforcement from those around us for behaving in a punitive, judgmental way, than in a way that is respectful to our children.[7]

PART V

NVC IN SOCIETY

Nonviolent Communication
is power *with* people.[21]

13

POWER AND PUNISHMENT

POWER-OVER OR POWER-WITH

NONVIOLENT COMMUNICATION IS power *with* people. [21]

NONVIOLENT COMMUNICATION OFFERS people caught up in domination systems a way of thinking and communicating that I'm sure would make their life much more wonderful. We can show them a game that's much more fun to play than dominating other people and creating wars. Really, there's a much more enjoyable way to live! [8]

NEVER GIVE PEOPLE, or the institutions within which we live, the power to make you submit or rebel. [10]

WE CAN NEVER make anyone do anything against their will without enormous consequences. [34]

WHENEVER OUR OBJECTIVE is to get somebody to stop doing something, we lose power. [8]

～

POWER-OVER LEADS TO punishment and violence. Power-with leads to compassion and understanding, and to learning motivated by reverence for life rather than fear, guilt, shame, or anger. [34]

～

NONVIOLENT COMMUNICATION IS based on a concept of power, power with people. We want people to do things because they see how it's going to enrich life. That's power-*with*—when we have the ability to motivate people from within. In contrast, power-*over* gets people to do things because of their fear of what we're going to do to them if they don't meet our demands, or how we will reward them if they do.

My own children have taught me very early in life the danger of power-*over* tactics. One of the first things they taught me is I couldn't make them do anything. I can't tell you what a helpful lesson that was. Somehow in my jackal background, I got it in mind that it was the job of a teacher or a parent to get people to do what's right. But here's this two-year-old teaching me that no matter what I thought, I couldn't make them do anything. . . . All I could do is make them wish they had.

And then they taught me a second lesson about power. Anytime I made them wish they had, they would make me wish I hadn't made them wish they had. Said more simply, violence begets violence. Anytime I used violence to get my way, I would pay for it. [10]

～

ONE FINAL DISTINCTION we need to be clear about is the concept of power-over versus power-with. Power over others gets things done by making people submit. You can punish, or you can reward. That's power-*over*. It's very weak power because you have to pay for it. Research shows that companies, families, or schools that use power-over tactics pay for it indirectly through morale problems, violence, and subtle actions against the system.

Power-*with* is getting people to do things willingly, because they see how it's going to enrich everybody's well-being by doing it. That's Nonviolent Communication. One of the most powerful ways we've found of creating power *with* people is the degree to which we show them we're just as interested in their needs as our own.

We create more power *with* people to the degree that we evaluate honestly and vulnerably without criticism. People are much more concerned about our well-being when we share power than when we tell them what's wrong with them. [8]

~

WE GET THIS kind of power, power *with* people, by being able to openly communicate our feelings and needs without in any way criticizing the other person. We do that by offering them what we would like from them in a way that is not heard as demanding or threatening. And as I have said, it also requires really hearing what other people are trying to communicate, showing an accurate understanding rather than quickly jumping in and giving advice, or trying to fix things. [7]

~

AT THE ROOT of every tantrum and power struggle are unmet needs. [34]

~

THE WORD *OBEDIENCE* describes how we sometimes choose to do what the authorities request because we see how it serves life. And I wouldn't then call that *obedience* to authority. I would say I'm choosing to do what the authority says because it's in harmony with my needs. [3]

~

WHEN RULES ARE established by the people who are going to be affected by them, not handed down unilaterally by some authority, and everyone sees that the intention is to protect, not to punish, these rules are more likely to be respected. This is true regardless of peoples' ages. [4]

⤳

HOW CONCERNED AM I about thinking we have to be afraid of what other people might say or think about us? By doing that, we're giving our power to other people. I tried to show people that we need to be concerned with how we respond to the other person, not what they think of us. [31]

PUNISHMENT AND REWARD

PUNISHMENT IS THE root of violence on our planet. [34]

⤳

USE PUNISHMENT IF you want to make a worse world. Punish children, support governments that punish criminals. [29]

⤳

VIOLENCE COMES FROM the belief that other people cause our pain and therefore deserve punishment. [34]

⤳

PUNISHMENT ALSO INCLUDES judgmental labeling and the withholding of privileges. [34]

⤳

BLAMING AND PUNISHING others are superficial expressions of anger. [34]

WE'VE BEEN EDUCATED to think in terms of rewards and punishment instead of what's alive in us and what would make life more wonderful. [8]

~

THERE ARE WHOLE cultures that have never been educated to use punishment. . . . They don't know what you mean by it. It doesn't exist. . . . If somebody in the tribe kills or rapes someone, the assumption is not that their evil is coming out and they have to be punished for it. It's, "My God, this person must have forgotten what the best game in town is. What's the best game in town? We all know that it's contributing to one another's well-being. This person must have forgotten." So, they put this person down in the middle of the circle and all day long people remind him of all of the things he's done that have enriched the lives of other people. [24]

~

IF YOU BELIEVE the story we've been told—that human beings are basically evil and selfish until they are crushed or controlled by the virtuous forces—then you have a person given the power to use punishment with people who are designated evil and to reward those who are good. [3]

~

I LEARNED THAT it is much more natural for people to connect in a loving, respectful way, and to do things out of joy for one another, rather than using punishment and reward or blame and guilt as means of coercion. But such a transformation does require a good deal of consciousness and effort. [7]

~

YOU SEE, WITH NVC ears we never hear what a person doesn't want. We try to help them get clear what they do want. Being clear only about what we don't want is a dangerous phenomenon. It gets us into all kinds of confusion.

When we are clear on what we do want from other people, especially when we are clear about what we want their reasons to be in doing something, then it becomes clear to us that we can never get our needs met through any kind of threats or punitive measures. Whether we are parents, teachers, or whatever, we never get our needs met by punishment. No one who is the least bit conscious is going to want anyone to do anything for us out of fear, guilt, or shame. We're NVC-oriented enough to see into the future, to see that anytime anyone does anything out of fear, guilt, or shame, everybody loses. [1]

⌇

IT'S ALWAYS VIRTUOUS punishment in a jackal culture. Nobody ever says, "I'm going to punish you 'cause I got pissed off." That's more honest. No, in a jackal culture I only punish you because I love you. That's painful. . . . Punishing people in the name of virtue, that's dangerous. [23]

⌇

THE MORE WE punish a person, the more violent they become. So if I really do want this person to behave less violently, the last thing I want to do is punish them for the violence. But nor do I want to be permissive, because doing nothing increases the violence. So permissiveness and punitiveness both increase the violence. [14]

⌇

GIVING PEOPLE AN option to willingly serve life is a far more powerful way to motivate people than reward or punishment. The only time we need to use punishment and reward is to oppress people— when what you're asking them to do doesn't serve life, but it serves the shareholders. [26]

⌇

SO, IF YOU want to educate people to be nice, dead people within hierarchical structures, it's critically important that you teach them that punishment and reward are justified. [3]

⮑

REWARDS AND PUNISHMENT are not necessary when people see how their efforts are contributing to their own well-being and the well-being of others. [4]

⮑

WHEN WE SUBMIT to doing something solely for the purpose of avoiding punishment, our attention is distracted from the value of the action itself. Instead, we are focusing upon the consequences, on what might happen if we fail to take that action. [5]

⮑

Two Questions That Reveal the Limitations of Punishment

LET'S STRIVE FOR no punishment from this point on. Punishment is at the root of violence on our planet. There are ways of maintaining social rules and regulations that do not involve any kind of punishment. If we ask two questions of ourselves, we will see that punishment never works.

First question: What do we want the other person to do? Now, if we ask only that question, one can make an argument for punishment. You can probably think of times when you know that somebody was influenced to do something either by being punished for what they had done or out of a threat of punishment. However, when we add the second question, we see that punishment never works.

What is the second question? What do we want the other person's reasons to be for doing as we request? [10]

> **Rewards and punishment
> are not necessary when people see
> how their efforts are contributing to
> their own well-being and the
> well-being of others.** [4]

NOW FOR MOST people raised in our culture, they can't imagine what a world would look like without punishment. They have horrible images of anarchy, chaos, a world where nothing would ever get done. It's a hard concept to let go of until you really get clear about those two questions. If you don't get clear about those two questions, you can often end up thinking punishment works when it really doesn't. [10]

〜

I BELIEVE THAT we'll see that punishment never can really get our needs met in a constructive way if we can ask ourselves two questions. The first question is: *What do we want the other person to do differently than what they are now doing?* If we ask only this question, at times punishment seems to work, because we may be able to get a child to stop hitting his sister if we punish him for doing it. I say it *seems to work,* because often the very act of punishing people for what they do in fact stimulates such antagonism that they continue to do it out of resentment or anger. They continue to do it longer than they would have done had there not been punishment.

But if we add a second question, I'm confident that we will then see that punishment never works in the sense of getting our needs met, for reasons that we won't be sorry for later. The second question is: *What do we want the other person's reasons to be for doing what we want them to do?*

When we ask that question, I think we will see that we never want other people to do things because they are afraid of punishment. We don't want people to do things out of obligation or duty, or out of guilt or shame, or to buy love. With some consciousness, I'm confident we would each see that we only want people to do things if they can do it willingly, because they clearly see how it's going to enrich life if they do. Any other reason for doing things is likely to create conditions that make it harder for people in the future to behave in a compassionate way toward one another. [9]

Reward

I THINK THAT there is a problem with rewards and consequences because in the long run, they rarely work in the ways we hope. In fact, they are likely to backfire. [34]

↬

PRAISE AND REWARD create a system of extrinsic motivations for behavior. Children (and adults) end up taking action in order to receive the praise or rewards. [34]

↬

I'D LIKE TO suggest that reward is just as coercive as punishment. In both cases we are using power *over* people, controlling the environment in a way that tries to force people to behave in ways that we like. In that respect, reward comes out of the same mode of thinking as punishment. [7]

↬

MANY PEOPLE BELIEVE that it's more humane to use reward than punishment. But both of them I see as power *over* others, and Nonviolent Communication is based on power *with* people. And in power *with* people, we try to have influence not by how we can make people suffer if they don't do what we want, or how we can reward them if they do. It's a power based on mutual trust and respect, which makes people open to hearing one another and learning from one another, and to giving to one another willingly out of a desire to contribute to one another's well-being, rather than out of a fear of punishment or hope for a reward. [7]

Restorative Justice

I HOPE THAT by now everybody is aware of the failure of the punitive structures that are part of our judicial system. There needs to be a transition from *retributive* justice to *restorative* justice. [8]

WE WANT TO restore the situation by replacing whatever education led to this person behaving as they did with an education that supports their contributing to people's well-being, rather than doing things which create suffering for people. [31]

~

WHAT DO WE do if we're around people who behave in ways that we find repugnant, even frightening? How do we change these individuals or get them to change? Here's where we really need to learn to apply *restorative* justice. We need to learn not to punish people when they behave in ways we don't like.

As I've said earlier, punishment is a losing game. We want people to change behavior, not because they're going to be punished if they continue, but because they see other options that better meet their needs at less cost. [8]

PROTECTIVE USE OF FORCE

THE PUNITIVE USE of force tends to generate hostility and to reinforce resistance to the very behavior we are seeking. [34]

~

THE INTENTION BEHIND the protective use of force is to prevent injury, never to punish or to cause individuals to suffer, repent, or change. [34]

~

WHEN WE EXERCISE the protective use of force, we are focusing on the life or rights we want to protect, without passing judgment on either the person or the behavior. [5]

~

GIRAFFES KNOW THE difference between the protective use of force and the punitive use of force. I can grab a child and hold them. That's protective use of force; I'm not doing this to punish this person. I'm doing it to protect another person from the violence. I can do that without hitting the person. [14]

∽

THE INTENTION BEHIND the protective use of force is to prevent injury or injustice. The intention behind the punitive use of force is to cause individuals to suffer for their perceived misdeeds. [5]

∽

ONE WAY TO differentiate between the protective and punitive use of force is to examine what the person using force is thinking. A person using the protective use of force is not judging the other person in a moralistic way. Instead his thinking is focused on protecting the well-being of himself and/or others. [4]

∽

IN THE PUNITIVE use of force, it is our intent to create pain and suffering for the other person, to make them sorry for what they did. In the protective use of force, our intent is only to protect. We protect our needs, and then later we'll have the communication necessary to educate the person. [7]

∽

ONE WAY OF remembering the purpose of the protective use of force is to see the difference between controlling the child and controlling the environment. In punishment we're trying to control the child by making the child feel bad about what they've done, to create an internal shame, guilt, or fear for what they have done.

In the protective use of force, our intent is not to control the child; it's to control the environment. To protect our needs until such time as we can have the quality of communication with the other person that's really necessary.[7]

᳂

THE ASSUMPTION BEHIND the protective use of force is that people behave in ways injurious to themselves and others due to some form of ignorance. The corrective process is therefore one of education, not punishment. Ignorance includes (1) a lack of awareness of the consequences of our actions, (2) an inability to see how our needs may be met without injury to others, (3) the belief that we have the right to punish or hurt others because they "deserve" it, and (4) delusional thinking that involves, for example, hearing a voice that instructs us to kill someone.[5]

᳂

THE PROTECTIVE USE of force is based on the assumption that people do things that harm themselves and/or others out of ignorance. This ignorance might be in the form of not knowing how one's actions are affecting others, ignorance of how to meet one's own needs without violating the needs of others, or culturally learned ignorance that justifies violating the needs of others (for example, to justify one's belief that others deserve to suffer for what they have done).

Another way to differentiate between the protective and punitive use of force is by examining the intention of the person using the force. The intention of someone using the protective use of force is to prevent injury or violation of someone's rights.[4]

᳂

LET'S SET BOUNDARIES. It's very important, but not [only] for children. For any human being. Any human being who is violating a need of yours and is unwilling to negotiate about it, tell them what you're going to do. And do it. Use protective use of force. But do that with everybody. Don't think that's just with children. We all need clarity. [22]

14

LEARNING THAT SERVES LIFE

HOW TO LEARN

I CAN'T RECALL seriously learning anything by being told what I am. [5]

∽

EVERY TIME I do something that doesn't meet my needs, I want to use it as an opportunity to grow and learn. . . . The main thing we need to do is to get clear what the new option is. [22]

∽

I'M INTERESTED IN learning that's motivated by reverence for life, that's motivated by a desire to learn skills, to learn new things that help us to better contribute to our own well-being and the well-being of others. And what fills me with great sadness is any learning that I see motivated by coercion. [10]

∽

LEARNING IS TOO precious to be motivated by coercive tactics. [34]

ANY LEARNING WE do that comes from self-blame is very costly. Because we may now develop some better way of handling a situation, but if we got there by blaming ourselves, we have tarnished our consciousness of our divine energy. We are divine energy. We don't want to ever lose that consciousness that we are divine energy. [12]

⤸

IF THE WAY we evaluate ourselves leads us to feel shame, and we consequently change our behavior, we are allowing our growing and learning to be guided by self-hatred. Shame is a form of self-hatred, and actions taken in reaction to shame are not free and joyful acts. Even if our intention is to behave with more kindness and sensitivity, if people sense shame or guilt behind our actions, they are less likely to appreciate what we do than if we are motivated purely by the human desire to contribute to life. [5]

⤸

WE USE NVC to evaluate ourselves in ways that engender growth rather than self-hatred. [34]

⤸

WE SOMETIMES BEHAVE in a way that doesn't meet our needs. So we want to learn from this without losing connection with our consciousness of our divine energy. So that requires that we learn how to mourn when we have not met our needs, without blaming ourselves. Without thinking that there's anything wrong with us. There is nothing wrong with us. There never has been, there never will be. We've done some things we wouldn't have done if we knew then what we're learning now. [12]

⤸

WE NEED TO learn, but without hating ourselves. Learning that occurs through guilt or shame is costly learning. It's too late now to undo that learning. We have it within ourselves. We've been trained to educate ourselves with violent judgments.

We show you in our training how to catch yourself when you're talking to yourself like that and to bring those judgments into the light, to see what you're telling yourself. You realize that this is your way of educating yourself—to call yourself names, to think of what's wrong with you. Then we show you how to look behind these judgments to the need at the root of them. That is to say, what need of yours wasn't met by the behavior? [8]

⤔

IT IS TRAGIC that so many of us get enmeshed in self-hatred rather than benefit from our mistakes, which show us our limitations and guide us toward growth. [5]

⤔

WHEN WE MAKE mistakes, we can use the process of NVC mourning and self-forgiveness to show us where we can grow instead of getting caught up in moralistic self-judgments. [34]

⤔

THE VAST MAJORITY of people we call mentally ill are simply "well-educated" to think and communicate in a way that causes them great psychological discomfort. It doesn't mean they're ill; it means they've learned ways of thinking and communicating that make life pretty miserable.

So, our first step in helping people is to show them how to learn from their mistakes without losing self-respect. Or, as I say it in my Detroit way, how to enjoy mucking things up. [8]

⤔

PRACTICE THE WAY you'd like to respond differently, then empathize with yourself. What kept you from doing that? This is how you celebrate the muckups. You learn without hating yourself. [31]

THE MOST CRUCIAL application of NVC may be in the way we treat ourselves. When we make mistakes, instead of getting caught up in moralistic self-judgments, we can use the process of NVC mourning and self-forgiveness to show us where we can grow. By assessing our behaviors in terms of our own unmet needs, the impetus for change comes not out of shame, guilt, anger, or depression, but out of the genuine desire to contribute to our own and others' well-being.

We also cultivate self-compassion by consciously choosing in daily life to act only in service to our own needs and values rather than out of duty, for extrinsic rewards, or to avoid guilt, shame, and punishment. If we review the joyless acts to which we currently subject ourselves and make the translation from "have to" to "choose to," we will discover more play and integrity in our lives. [5]

⤝

WHEN WE COMMUNICATE with ourselves on a regular basis through inner judgment, blame, and demand, it's not surprising that our self-concept gives in to feeling more like a chair than a human being. A basic premise of NVC is that whenever we imply that someone is wrong or bad, what we are really saying is that he or she is not acting in harmony with our needs. If the person we are judging happens to be ourselves, what we are saying is, "I myself am not behaving in harmony with my own needs." I am convinced that if we learn to evaluate ourselves in terms of whether and how well our needs are being fulfilled, we are much more likely to learn from the evaluation.

Our challenge then, when we are doing something that is not enriching life, is to evaluate ourselves moment by moment in a way that inspires change both (1) in the direction of where we would like to go, and (2) out of respect and compassion for ourselves, rather than out of self-hatred, guilt, or shame. [5]

⤝

AN IMPORTANT ASPECT of self-compassion is to be able to empathically hold both parts of ourselves—the self that regrets a past action and the self that took the action in the first place. The process of mourning and self-forgiveness frees us in the direction of learning and growing. In connecting moment by moment to our needs, we increase our creative capacity to act in harmony with them. [5]

⤚⤙

WHAT DO WE need to do to support this person learning a different way? Look at how we are educating people, and make sure we are educating people to see that our well-being is one and the same, that we can never meet our own needs at other people's expense. [31]

⤚⤙

OUR MOST UGLY, aggravating jackal is our best guru. See, we stand more to benefit, more to learn from those people whose beauty we cannot see than anybody else. They're our best teachers. [22]

APOLOGY

ANY APOLOGY THAT comes out of thinking you did something wrong is not going to be good for you or the other person. [33]

⤚⤙

NOT FOR ONE second do we ever want to think we do anything wrong; it's impossible. You can't do anything wrong. Even if you try, you couldn't do anything wrong. You didn't meet your own needs to be sensitive. So, out of that kind of mourning comes learning without self-hatred. But apology, whatever learning happens, has the taint of self-hatred associated with it. [16]

LET'S LOOK AT the difference between mourning and apology more closely. Apology is based on moralistic judgment, that what I did was wrong and I should suffer for it, even hate myself for what I did. That's radically different than mourning, which is not based on moralistic judgments. Mourning is based on life-serving judgments. Did I meet my own needs? No. Then what need didn't I meet? [2]

⤺

APOLOGY IS BASICALLY part of our violent language. It implies wrongness—that you should be blamed, that you should be penitent, that you're a terrible person for what you did—and when you agree that you are a horrible person and when you have become sufficiently penitent, you can be forgiven. *Sorry* is part of that game. If you hate yourself enough, you can be forgiven, you see.

Now, in contrast, what is really healing for people is not that game where we agree that we're terrible, but rather going inside yourself and seeing what need of yours was not met by the behavior. And when you are in touch with that, you feel a different kind of suffering. You feel a natural suffering, a kind of suffering that leads to learning and healing, not to hatred of oneself, not to guilt. [8]

⤺

MOST OF THE time people think they want an apology or vengeance. Their real need is for empathy for their suffering. I've yet to see a person who's gotten real empathy for their suffering that still wants an apology. [22]

⤺

MOST OF THE time we're apologizing to another person, but we haven't even empathized with them first. We don't realize that when we start apologizing in a jackal way, before we've even given empathy to the other person's suffering, we're apologizing to get forgiveness for ourselves, and we're adding insult to injury to the other person. [30]

NO APOLOGY, IN whatever form, is trusted until we feel that that person has first empathized. Otherwise it's just a ritual, designed for the other person to get forgiven. [30]

~

WHEN WE SPEAK giraffe we don't live in the world of right and wrong. We do what Rumi the poet says, that there's a place beyond right- and wrongdoing. "I'll meet you there." That world of right- and wrongdoing is where all the violence is created. Apology is part of that game. But I mourn if I see that my behavior is not enriching life. I mourn. But that's a radically different world to live in than that of right- and wrongdoing. [26]

MOURN AND CELEBRATE

LIFE FOR A giraffe is constant celebration. We're either celebrating how life has been enriched or how it can be. See, all giraffes like to do is play. [22]

~

MANY PEOPLE HAVE trouble celebrating what they do. They've been programmed to think in terms of how it could be done better. [27]

~

EVERYTHING THAT EVERY human being has ever done is out of holy purposes, to make life more wonderful. Now, sometimes our actions fulfill our needs to make life more wonderful and sometimes they don't. We need to celebrate when they do and mourn when they don't. Any kind of self-blame will interfere with the learning. [22]

~

" If we want to learn from our limitations, without losing self-respect, it's critical that we learn how to mourn without blame. [19] "

THE TWO THINGS we need to do well, I believe, and what Nonviolent Communication is designed to help us with, is to mourn and celebrate. When we have done something that enriches life, how to really get connected to how our needs were fulfilled and to feel the good feelings that come about as a result of that. Celebration of life is very important. And the other side is equally important; when we've done something that didn't enrich life, to feel the pain that comes naturally from the need that wasn't met. [19]

⌣

IF WE WANT to learn from our limitations, without losing self-respect, it's critical that we learn how to mourn without blame. [19]

⌣

WHEN WE GET in touch with needs of ours that weren't met by our behavior, I call that mourning—mourning our actions. But it's mourning without blame, mourning without thinking there's something wrong with us for doing what we did. [8]

⌣

MOURNING IS A celebration in a sense. It's an awakening up to life. It's seeing how life wasn't met but that means it's a possibility to better serve life, you see. That's where the learning comes in. [15]

⌣

MOURN OUR LIMITATIONS as human beings. We often behave in ways that do not get our needs met. We need to learn how to go deeply into that; not be afraid to face the depth of suffering. But we have to watch out that we don't get stuck by scattering judgments, like, "What's wrong with me for always doing this?" This kind of static thinking blocks the natural flow. [18]

⌣

THE TRUTH IS you had a need that wasn't met by that behavior. And hearing that need I'm predicting will more likely lead you to fulfill the need in other ways that are more effective and less costly than thinking you did anything wrong. That's giraffe mourning. Especially if we can combine the mourning with the next step which is empathizing with the part of yourself that did it. What needs were being met by doing it? [15]

⮑

I'VE ASKED PEOPLE who have been blaming themselves for mistakes they've made to get in touch with how that feels, and then compare it to how it feels with mourning, where instead of thinking what you did is wrong just to be clear what need wasn't met, and how do you feel about that. It amazes me how often people use the word *sweet* to identify the pain when we're fully connected to the need that wasn't met. And that's mourning. It didn't meet my need for this, and I feel this as a result. That's a sweet pain, compared to "How could I do such a stupid thing, what's wrong with me?" [19]

⮑

WHEN WE DO something we don't like, the first step is to mourn, to empathize with ourselves about the need of ours that wasn't met. And very often we'll have to do that by "hearing through" the judgments we have been programmed to make. In this way, we can actually make good use of our depression, guilt, and shame. We can use those feelings as an alarm clock to wake us up to the fact that at this moment we really are not connected to life—life defined as being in touch with our needs. We're up in our head playing violent games with ourselves, calling ourselves names.

If we can learn how to empathically connect with the need of ours that wasn't met, and then look at the part of our self that was trying to meet the need, we're better prepared to see what's alive in ourselves and others—and to take the steps necessary to make life more wonderful.

Often it's not easy to empathically connect with that need. If we look inside and say what was going on in us when we did that, very often we say things to ourselves like "I had to do it; I had no choice." That's never true! We always have a choice. We don't do anything we didn't choose to do. We chose to behave that way to meet a need. A very important part of Nonviolent Communication is this recognition of choice at every moment, that every moment we choose to do what we do, and we don't do anything that isn't coming out of choice. What's more, every choice we make is in the service of a need. That's how Nonviolent Communication works within us. [8]

AFTER A LIFETIME of schooling and socialization, it is probably too late for most of us to train our minds to think purely in terms of what we need and value from moment to moment. However, just as we have learned to translate judgments when conversing with others, we can train ourselves to recognize judgmental self-talk and to immediately focus our attention on the underlying needs. [5]

MOURNING IN NVC is the process of fully connecting with the unmet needs and the feelings that are generated when we have been less than perfect. It is an experience of regret, but regret that helps us learn from what we have done without blaming or hating ourselves. We see how our behavior ran counter to our own needs and values, and we open ourselves to feelings that arise out of that awareness. When our consciousness is focused on what we need, we are naturally stimulated toward creative possibilities for how to get that need met. In contrast, the moralistic judgments we use when blaming ourselves tend to obscure such possibilities and to perpetuate a state of self-punishment. [5]

WE FOLLOW UP on the process of mourning with self-forgiveness. Turning our attention to the part of the self which chose to act in the way that led to the present situation, we ask ourselves, "When I behaved in the way which I now regret, what need of mine was I trying to meet?" I believe that human beings are always acting in the service of needs and values. This is true whether the action does or does not meet the need, or whether it's one we end up celebrating or regretting.

When we listen empathically to ourselves, we will be able to hear the underlying need. Self-forgiveness occurs the moment this empathic connection is made. Then we are able to recognize how our choice was an attempt to serve life, even as the mourning process teaches us how it fell short of fulfilling our needs. 5

ONCE I'M CONSCIOUS of the needs and not thinking of what's wrong with me, I'm much more likely to meet my needs. But if I think that I am basically a rat's ass for not meeting my wife's needs better, I'll continue to behave like a rat's ass. What you see is what you get. If I see other people as selfish, don't expect me to act toward them in a way that they will enjoy giving to. But if I mourn, I'm much more likely to figure out ways of getting my needs met, because my consciousness is on what needs aren't getting met, not what's wrong with me. 12

15

EDUCATING OUR CHILDREN

WE HAVE BEEN educated to work for extrinsic rewards, not to look at whether what we're doing is serving life. [22]

⤷

UNFORTUNATELY, WE WERE educated in guilt-inducing ways by authorities—teachers, parents, etc.—who used guilt to mobilize us to do what they wanted. [8]

SCHOOLING

THE PROBLEM WITH people who are in touch with their needs is that they do not make good slaves. I went to schools for twenty-one years, and I can't recall ever being asked what my needs were. My education didn't focus on helping me be more alive, more in touch with myself and others. It was oriented toward rewarding me for giving right answers as defined by authorities. [8]

⤷

U.S. SCHOOLS, HOWEVER, are doing what they were set up to do, which is to support gang behavior. Which gang? In this case, it's the economic-structure gang, the people who control our businesses. They control our schools, and they have three historical goals:

First, to teach people obedience to authority so that when they get hired they'll do what they're told.

Second, they get people to work for extrinsic rewards. They want people to learn not how to enrich their lives, but to receive grades, to be rewarded with a better high-paying job in the future. If you're a gang who wants to hire a person to put out a product or service that doesn't really serve life (but makes a lot of money for the owners of this gang), you want workers who aren't asking themselves, "Is this product we're turning out really serving life?" No, you just want them to do what they're told and to work for a salary.

[Educational historian Michael B.] Katz says the third function of our schools—and this really makes lasting change difficult—is that they're doing a good job of maintaining a caste system and making it look like a democracy. [8]

TEACHING IN A public school is like being a car salesman; if this salesman doesn't make any sales, you fire the customer. Isn't that how it is in the schools? If the teacher doesn't do his or her job, the student gets blamed. The student is a slow learner, the student is bipolar, this student has attention deficit disorder, this person is culturally deprived, this person is this, this is that. You always fire the customer. [18]

LANGUAGE IS A critical way of molding people's minds. You can control people's minds to a large extent by the language you put in their heads. So, it's very important that some of the first words you want to get people to hear are the words *good, bad, right, wrong, normal, abnormal,*

should, shouldn't, have to, and *can't.* If you want people to be controllable by authority, the key unit of education is language. [3]

❧

AS WITH ALL Life-Enriching interactions, what makes the resolution mutual is the teacher's consciousness that the objective is not to get the student to do what the teacher wants, but to create the quality of connection that will allow both the teacher and the student to get their needs met. [4]

❧

WHEN WE HAVE our consciousness so focused on what people might think of us, and what we think of ourselves if we make mistakes, then any kind of learning is frightening. That's why about 15 percent of students follow the philosophy, you can't fall out of bed if you sleep on the floor. Many of those we call underachievers are so fearful of not getting things right, they have decided it's easier and safer not to do anything. [4]

❧

SO WHEN WE train people to hear criticism and negative judgment, any kind of learning is about as much fun as a prolonged dental appointment. Hearing criticism in what people say, or worrying about what people think of you—whether you are smart or dumb, right or wrong—has terrible effects on how we see ourselves. We don't see ourselves as beautiful. We can't.

Schooling teaches us—and taught me—to dehumanize human beings by thinking of *what* they are. And so I've been working very hard to develop this other language that helps me to stay connected to the beauty in people. [10]

❧

LIFE-ENRICHING EDUCATION

WE RECOGNIZE THAT real educational reform is essential if today's and tomorrow's children are to live in a more peaceful, just, and sustainable world. [34]

⌒

THOUGH THE ROAD to educational innovation is not easy, I see it as a powerful way to ever achieve peace on this planet. If future generations can be educated in schools structured so that everyone's needs are valued, I believe they will be better able to create life-enriching families, workplaces, and governments. [4]

⌒

I'M INTERESTED IN learning that's motivated by reverence for life, that's motivated by a desire to learn skills, to learn new things that help us to better contribute to our own well-being and the well-being of others.

And what fills me with great sadness is any learning that I see motivated by coercion. By coercion I mean the following: Any student that's learning anything out of a fear of punishment, out of a desire for rewards in the form of grades, to escape guilt or shame, or out of some vague sense of "ought" or "must" or "should." Learning is too precious, I believe, to be motivated by any of these coercive tactics. [10]

⌒

USING NONVIOLENT COMMUNICATION skills, constantly asking of students, teachers, administrators, and ourselves, "What are you feeling and needing?" we actually can meet everyone's needs. No longer will the goal be merely to reduce violence and vandalism, to keep kids in school as long as possible, to get higher scores on the proficiency tests than the kids in the next county do, to get more kids into college than we did last year, or to improve our students' showing on the SAT exams.

> **We recognize that real educational reform is essential if today's and tomorrow's children are to live in a more peaceful, just, and sustainable world.** [34]

No longer will students and teachers alike be given only two choices, to submit or rebel. When there is only one goal, to get everyone's needs met, classrooms and schools can be transformed. Because what we discover is that everyone's needs are the same. [4]

⤶

I WOULD LIKE to educate this and future generations of children to create new organizations whose goal is to meet human needs—to make life more wonderful for themselves and others. I call the process of education that can achieve this, Life-Enriching Education. I call its opposite Domination Education. [4]

⤶

ONCE WE ARE aware of the power of domination systems, it is easier to see that a transformation to life-enriching systems offers a better opportunity to meet the needs of all our citizens. I would like to educate this and future generations of children to create organizations whose goal is to meet human needs, to make life more wonderful for themselves and each other. From that awareness, we can use the education of our children as a place to start. [4]

⤶

LIFE-ENRICHING EDUCATION: AN education that prepares children to learn throughout their lives, relate well to others, and themselves, be creative, flexible, and venturesome, and have empathy not only for their immediate kin but for all of humankind. [34]

⤶

LIFE-ENRICHING CLASSROOMS AND schools are likely to be struggling within school systems whose purpose is unfortunately not supportive of them. In any domination system the goal, unwittingly or otherwise, is to perpetuate the status quo—an economic system in which a few people maintain their wealth and privilege while others remain permanently in or near poverty.

Such systems are not going to respond positively in the long term to the kind of educational innovations that I propose. It may be possible to launch new educational programs, but unless we organize ongoing teams of people to sustain them, the schools are likely to soon revert back to their original structures and procedures. [4]

⤳

PUBLIC EDUCATION FOR some time has been heavily focused on what curricula we believe will be helpful to students. Life-Enriching Education is based on the premise that the relationship between teachers and students, the relationships of students with one another, and the relationships of students to what they are learning are equally important in preparing students for the future.

Children need far more than basic skills in reading, writing, and math, as important as those might be. Children also need to learn how to think for themselves, how to find meaning in what they learn, and how to work and live together. Teachers, school administrators, and parents will come away from Life-Enriching Education with skills in language, communication, and ways of structuring the learning environment that support the development of autonomy and interdependence in the classroom. [4]

⤳

AS TEACHERS, WE can prepare students for participating in and creating life-enriching organizations by speaking a language that allows us to truly connect with one another moment by moment. I call this language Nonviolent Communication. By speaking this language we can make partners of teachers and students, give students the tools with which to settle their disputes without fighting, build bridges between former adversaries such as parents and school boards, and contribute to our own well-being and the well-being of others. [4]

BUILT INTO NONVIOLENT Communication is a language of choice. To be conscious, don't do anything you don't choose to do, don't choose to do anything that isn't to serve life. Don't do anything for reward, don't do anything to escape punishment, don't do anything out of guilt, out of shame, duty, obligation. So, we want anything done in the school to come out of choice, because they see how it's going to enrich life. [18]

⸌⸍

FIRST THING WE do is we want to teach these students how to work for intrinsic motives, not extrinsic. If you don't see how something is going to enrich your life, why do it? If you don't see how it's going to serve life, why do it? [18]

⸌⸍

I'M SUGGESTING TODAY that we never evaluate a student's performance by any jackal language. Let's get the following words out of our consciousness as teachers: *right, wrong, good, bad, correct, incorrect, slow learner, fast learner.* This is dangerous language. [10]

⸌⸍

GUILT IS A form of violence as I define violence. We don't allow punishment by guilt in Nonviolent Communication schools we've created in different countries. These are disallowed tactics for resolving any differences. Punishment, reward, guilt. [10]

⸌⸍

STUDENTS EDUCATED IN such a judgment-free environment learn because they choose to, not to earn rewards or avoid moralistic judgments or punishment. Every teacher knows, or at least can imagine, the joy of teaching a student who truly wants to learn, an experience that is all too rare. [4]

⸌⸍

STUDENTS RECEIVE POWERFUL learning experiences from the ways their classrooms and schools are organized. The organization of classrooms and schools can support the learning necessary for students to develop and maintain either structures that support interdependence or structures that support competition and domination.

Life-Enriching Education structures the school as a community where each student is equally concerned about contributing to other students' reaching their learning objectives as they are about reaching their own. [4]

∽

SCHOOLS AND CLASSROOMS where interdependent learning communities are thriving usually encourage students who have reached certain objectives, to assist others wishing to reach these objectives. [4]

∽

I BELIEVE THAT the apathy characteristic in many classrooms can be largely traced to a lack of commitment by the students to the objectives toward which they are working. In fact, as has been mentioned, in many cases the students are not even clear as to what the objectives are. Industrial psychologists have documented the degree to which morale and productivity are related to commitment to objectives. I believe it is a mistake to begin any course of instruction before the teacher is convinced that each student is committed to the proposed objective. When students are actively committed to objectives, I also see discipline problems greatly reduced. The more the goals of the student and those of the teacher coincide, the less problem of control I would anticipate. [4]

∽

TO MAXIMIZE COMMITMENT from students to objectives, teachers must not only be sincerely aware of the life-enriching nature of the objectives recommended, but they must also be able to communicate how the objectives will be life-enriching to the students.

If and when students are unwilling to pursue certain objectives, teachers need these communication skills to help them understand the reasons for the student's unwillingness, so the teachers can determine whether there are ways of making the objectives more appealing; or through this understanding, the teacher might come to see that other objectives would be better for the student to pursue than the ones originally advocated by the teacher. [4]

෧

AFTER THE TEACHER and student have mutually established learning objectives, the teacher then works with students to obtain the information and materials they need to successfully fulfill the objectives. Ideally, the materials may be such that students often can use them by themselves. This involves the teacher identifying the prerequisite competencies or concepts that constitute readiness on the part of students to start working toward their objectives. [4]

෧

WE TEACH TEACHERS that style of leadership, the leader is servant. No punishment, no reward, no grades. Tests are given, but the tests are not of the students. Tests are given of the teachers. So, for example, if I'm a teacher and I offer you something, how do I know I did my job well without giving you a test? So I give you a test to see if I did my job well. I don't give you the test to grade you and rank you. [18]

෧

IN LIFE-ENRICHING EDUCATIONAL programs, tests are given to determine whether or not objectives have been reached, and if not, the tests provide information about what the student still needs to accomplish. Tests are not given at the end of instruction solely to determine grades.

Reporting on a student's progress in a Life-Enriching Education classroom is done by describing the competencies that a student has developed. . . . Grades are not given in Life-Enriching Educational programs. Instead, reports are presented about exactly what students are able to do at the end of the learning period that they were not able to do at the beginning. [4]

↜

IN LIFE-ENRICHING EDUCATION, whatever rules and regulations are needed to maintain order are decided on through dialogue by the staff and students working together, being respectful of everyone's needs. This process does not involve anyone giving in, giving up, or compromising.

To maintain order and resolve conflicts in this way requires the staff and students to be competent in Nonviolent Communication skills. Staff and students need to be literate in connecting with one another's feelings and needs. After this quality of connection is reached, both sides engage in problem-solving to find actions that can be taken that will fulfill all parties' needs.

It is important that before anyone agrees to carry out these actions that she checks inside to be sure she is motivated to act with the sole purpose of fulfilling needs, with no trace of doing anything to avoid punishment, guilt, or shame. Nor would she want to act out of a sense of duty or obligation, or in order to get a good grade or any other extrinsic reward. [4]

↜

IN OUR GIRAFFE schools, there's one thing we would like to teach students, if there's no other message: Be connected enough to your own spirituality so you don't let the structures determine how you behave. [29]

↜

THERE ARE MANY resources in our society that support individuals in their efforts to transform their lives. I would suggest to you that schools and other organizations can be similarly transformed—through the process and underlying principles of Nonviolent Communication. We can create a life-enriching system where all of us are given the chance to do what at heart we enjoy more than anything else: making life more wonderful for ourselves and others, meeting one another's needs. No matter what has happened in the past in a school or school system, if students and teachers and parents and administrators learn to connect in a life-enriching way, it is inevitable that they will start to create life-enriching communities.

I have seen it happen, time and again, and when it does, it's too beautiful for words. [4]

16

NVC AT WORK

WHEN WE WORK in a hierarchically structured institution, there is a tendency to hear commands and judgments from those higher up in the hierarchy. While we may easily empathize with our peers and with those in less powerful positions, we may find ourselves being defensive or apologetic, instead of empathic, in the presence of those we identify as our "superiors." [5]

~

IT'S NOT A matter of not having a conflict—it's how to use the conflict so you come out more powerful than if you didn't have the conflict. That's where our training really helps us within (the NVC organization). We apply our training and when we do, conflicts become something positive. If we don't apply our own training, it's useless. So we spend a lot of time dealing with conflict within our organization. [27]

~

THAT'S THE ESSENCE of Nonviolent Communication. To create connection between people so that everybody's needs get met and they get met through compassionate giving where people willingly want to give to one another. So, whether that is sales or if I'm an administrator in a company and an employee is behaving in a way I don't like, my objective in using Nonviolent Communication is not to get them to behave. It's to create a quality of connection necessary for everybody's needs to get met. [27]

PRODUCTIVITY

IN MANY CORPORATIONS, it's not easy to get people to talk at the level of needs and feelings, not to mention that they don't recognize what theologian Walter Wink says is important to know—that every institution, every organization has its own spirituality. And when the spirituality of the organization is "production over all," that's the only thing that counts. Human feelings, human needs, human*ness* don't matter. Then the company pays for it in terms of both morale and even production, because when you get people believing that their feelings and needs are understood, production will go up. [8]

～

YOU CAN HAVE high productivity and human connection. They're not in conflict. [27]

～

A LIFE-ENRICHING ORGANIZATION must be set up to be very good at getting genuine gratitude to every worker. That's the fuel necessary to keep people working in a life-enriching organization. [3]

～

MEETINGS

IF YOU WANT to make life easy for yourself and other people, you need to always be clear what you want back, anytime you say something to a person. And if you want to contribute to groups being unproductive, address a group that you're in this way: Start with "I think," and don't end on a request. Just say what you think, and . . . my prediction is, no matter what you started with, the meeting will be unproductive. [12]

‿つ

MY EXPERIENCE IS that it's not the people who are expressing emotions that are the problem in meetings; it's that they don't make clear what they want. [3]

‿つ

START ANY MEETING, where you have a lot resting on it with limited time, by requesting of the other person that they ask you what they need to know to give you what you want. [22]

‿つ

IF WE WANT to make meetings productive, we need to keep track of those whose requests are on the table. [34]

EVALUATION

AN ORGANIZATION THAT functions well, whether it be a family, school, business, is one in which I would say has constant ongoing performance evaluation. The more important the job, I think the more important we need constant evaluation. [27]

THE PEOPLE THAT I work with in the business area told me that they've actually gone to courses teaching them how to use gratitude and approval as a reward. They say research shows that if you compliment and praise employees daily production goes up. Yes, if you want to learn how to do that go to a dog obedience school. They'll show you how to use rewards and punishment to get performance. But it's dehumanizing for human beings to ever receive punishment or reward. [27]

MONEY

ABOVE ALL, NEVER do any work for money. . . . Get money to do the work that meets your need for meaning. [26]

～

I WANT MONEY, but I don't work for money. I work for the joy of serving life. . . . I ask people to give me money so I can have the nurturing to do the work. See, that means I have to really see what I'm doing—my work meets my need to serve life. I don't want to just be working at any job for the money. That's like hell on earth. To spend that many hours a day doing something for money. [27]

17

CHANGING OURSELVES AND OTHERS

WE'VE BEEN TELLING ourselves these jackal thoughts about ourselves our whole lives, because we've been educated to do it. After a lifetime of seeing ourselves in this way, how do we, beyond an abstract and intellectual level, really face the fact that we are created out of divine energy, that we have this enormous power? That's a pretty big jump, to go from being educated to believe that we're piss-poor protoplasm poorly put together, to seeing the truth. It's a pretty scary jump. [22]

↢

FOR MOST OF us the process of bringing about peaceful change begins with working on our own mindsets, on the way we view ourselves and others, on the way we get our needs met. This basic work is in many ways the most challenging aspect of speaking peace because it requires great honesty and openness, developing a certain literacy of expression, and overcoming deeply ingrained learning that emphasizes judgment, fear, obligation, duty, punishment and reward, and shame. It may not be easy, but the results are worth the effort. [8]

↢

THE MORE IMPORTANT it is that I want somebody to be open to another possibility, the more I want to begin with a respectful understanding with what need they're meeting by doing what they're doing. [22]

⤷

ONCE PEOPLE DON'T have to defend themselves against our single-mindedness of purpose to change them, once they feel understood for what they're doing, it's much easier for them to be open to other possibilities. [8]

⤷

SEE, A GIRAFFE-SPEAKING person—if you see somebody behaving in a way that you think is destructive for them—a giraffe-speaking person knows that the worst thing to do is try to help that person. To try to change them. That the only way to really get another person to change in a giraffe way is to give them a chance to nurture you, which means to really reveal your needs that would be met if they changed this behavior. [14]

⤷

HOW DO WE help a person get beyond any prejudice? Show them something that's more fun and less costly. [28]

⤷

I NEVER WANT to take anything away from people until I can show them something richer, better. [28]

⤷

WITH NVC, WE'RE trying to live a different value system while we are asking for things to change. What's most important is that every connection along the line mirrors the kind of world we're trying to

> "As we learn to speak
> from the heart, we are changing
> the habits of a lifetime. [34]

create. Each step needs to reflect energetically what we're after, which is a holographic image of the quality of relationships we're trying to create. In short, how we ask for change reflects the value system we're trying to support. [5]

⌇

AS WE LEARN to speak from the heart, we are changing the habits of a lifetime. [34]

18

SOCIAL CHANGE

SOCIAL CHANGE IS liberating ourselves from any theology, from any spirituality that is not in harmony with what we believe will enable us to create the kind of world we would like. [3]

↬

THE SPIRITUALITY THAT we need to develop for social change is one that mobilizes us for social change. It doesn't just enable us to sit there and enjoy the world no matter what. It creates a quality of energy that mobilizes us into action. [3]

↬

UNLESS WE AS social change agents come from a certain kind of spirituality, we're likely to create more harm than good. [34]

↬

I CAN TELL you a strategy that I'm trying to follow myself—the best that I've found at this point. It's this: Change the paradigm within myself, to liberate myself from the way I was programmed and to be in harmony with how I choose to live, with how I reflect the story that resonates the most in my heart. In other words, I strive to create that chosen world within. Peace begins with me. [3]

⤳

THAT'S ONE WAY to create social change. Share what works for us, what makes our lives richer without blasting the old paradigm, without calling them a bunch of bigots. . . . Tell what we like about our story, and how it's enriched our life. [3]

⤳

SOCIAL CHANGE INVOLVES helping people see new options for making life wonderful that are less costly to get needs met. [34]

⤳

IN MANY OF our social-change efforts, we are seemingly concerned with the actions of groups of people rather than individual behaviors. In my way of thinking, gangs are groups that behave in ways we don't like. Some gangs call themselves street gangs. They're not the ones that scare me the most.

Other gangs call themselves multinational corporations. Some gangs call themselves governments. These last two often do things as gangs that conflict with the values I embrace. These gangs control the schools, and many of them want the teachers to teach students that there's a right and a wrong, a good and a bad. They want schools to make students work for rewards so they can be hired later on to work eight hours a day for forty years of their life doing meaningless tasks. [8]

⤳

SO, THERE'S OBVIOUSLY enormous suffering created by gangs in our world. And it's pretty hard not to clean up the mess that these gangs create, but how and when do we focus on the gangs themselves that are creating the mess? So that, for me, is a major social change investment. To decide where I invest my energies. [3]

～

SOCIAL CHANGE REQUIRES a critical mass of people shifting from one way of getting their needs met to a different way. . . . That's what Nonviolent Communication is about, how to help people make a shift, from getting their needs met in a way that's violating other people, to finding a way to get everybody's needs met. So social change is basically just getting a significant number of people to shift from one place to another. [19]

～

WHEN IT COMES down to it, the biggest challenge in social-change efforts—whether in families, corporations, governments, or whatever—is getting people into the room together. I'm serious. This is the biggest challenge. [8]

～

WITH EACH PERSON that we connect with make sure it is our objective to create a certain quality of connection with that person. It's not to get what we want. We're really trying to live a different value system, even in our social change efforts, which means, yes, we would like to ask for some things, but what's most important to us is every connection along the line. Does it mirror the kind of world we're trying to create? Each step in every bit of asking we do needs to reflect energetically what we're after. It's a holographic image of the structure we're trying to create. In short, the asking process needs to reflect the value system we're trying to support. [3]

ONCE YOU HAVE access to key people in an organization, if you go into a meeting with enemy images of those people—if you think of them as bad, evil, maintaining the domination structures, or whatever—then you're not going to connect; in a sense you're part of the problem.[3]

&

WHEN WE USE this process of hearing what's alive in the other person, the other person cannot *not* communicate, because we hear every message coming from them verbally or nonverbally as an expression of what's alive in them. We sense their needs and feelings, and when we do that, we don't see any enemies, we don't see any resistance, and we don't see any criticism. We just see a human being that has the same needs that we have. We may not like their strategies for getting their needs met. But if we carry an enemy image of the people we're dealing with, I think we contribute to violence on the planet. So whatever social change I attempt, if it comes out of an enemy image that certain people are wrong or evil, I predict my attempts will be self-defeating.[3]

&

EFFECTIVE SOCIAL CHANGE requires connections with others in which we avoid seeing the people within these structures as enemies— and we try to hear the needs of the human beings within. Then we persist in keeping the flow of communication going so that everybody's needs get met.[8]

&

I WOULD LIKE to suggest that when our heads are filled with judgments and analyses that others are bad, greedy, irresponsible, lying, cheating, polluting the environment, valuing profit more than life, or behaving in other ways they shouldn't, very few of them will be interested in our needs. If we want to protect the environment, and we go to a corporate executive with the attitude, "You know, you are really a killer of the planet, you have no right to abuse the land in this way," we have severely impaired our chances of getting our needs met. It is a rare human being who can maintain focus on our needs when we are expressing them through images of their wrongness. [34]

~⁀

ALL THE SOCIAL change efforts boil down to three words: ask, ask, ask. To reach all of your objectives you have to ask, ask, ask. And if you don't want to be the only one doing all of the asking, you got to ask some people to help you do some asking. [3]

~⁀

IF EVER WE needed to know how not to use too many words, it's in social change efforts. Time is of the essence. We're often going to have a very limited time to do an awful lot of work. [3]

~⁀

SOCIAL CHANGE, OF course, is going to involve considerable confrontation at times. We need to learn how to use Nonviolent Communication when we're up against people who are opposed to what we're after, but who don't know how to express themselves in a way that clearly communicates their feelings and needs. We need to know (under these confrontational conditions) how to hear people's feelings and needs, no matter how they're communicating. [8]

~⁀

ONE OF MY social change objectives for the last several years has been to do what I can to contribute to transforming our judicial system from one based on the concept of retributive justice to one based on restorative justice. [31]

GIVEN THE ENORMITY of the social change that confronts us—change that we would all like to see—the thing that I predict will give us the most hope and strength to make change happen is if we make sure that we learn how to celebrate. Let's build celebration into our lives and come from that. That's first. Otherwise we're going to get overwhelmed by the immensity. Out of a spirit of celebration I think we'll have the energy to do whatever it takes to bring about social change. [3]

PART VI

NVC AS A WAY OF LIFE

Every time I mess up is
a chance to practice.[34]

19

UNDERSTANDING OUR RESPONSIBILITY

THE BASIC MECHANISM of motivating by guilt is to attribute the responsibility for one's own feelings to others. . . . On the surface, taking responsibility for the feelings of others can easily be mistaken for positive caring. [5]

୭

TO REALLY GIVE other people what they need, the empathy and the nurturing that they need . . . we must be conscious that their pain has nothing to do with us. [14]

୭

THE MAIN THING is that I be conscious that I'm never the cause of the other person's pain, but I do want to take responsibility for my behavior. See, I'm responsible for what I did. The other person is responsible for how they took it. [22]

୭

NVC . . . FOSTERS A level of moral development based on autonomy and interdependence, whereby we acknowledge responsibility for our own actions and are aware that our own well-being and that of others are one and the same. [5]

⤴

WE ARE RESPONSIBLE for what we hear other people say and for how we act. [34]

⤴

THE VERY WORD *responsible* means *response able*—able to respond. So, I cannot take responsibility for something over which I have no control. [22]

⤴

I WOULD LIKE all of us to take full responsibility for two things: our actions and our feelings. Actually, the feelings are also caused by our actions, our thinking. How we choose to interpret things. So we're responsible for our actions and for the thinking that causes our feelings. So nobody can make us do anything, nobody can make us angry, and nobody can hurt us. [19]

⤴

OTHER PEOPLE CAN'T make us feel anything. Our feelings are a result of how we take things. We cannot make other people feel as they do. They are responsible for how they take it. We show we're not responsible for how other people feel. We are responsible for our actions. [31]

⤴

COMMUNICATION IS LIFE-ALIENATING when it clouds our awareness that we are each responsible for our own thoughts, feelings, and actions. The use of the common expression *have to*, as in "There are some things you have to do, whether you like it or not," illustrates how personal responsibility for our actions can be obscured in speech. [5]

> " We are responsible for
> what we hear other people say
> and for how we act. [34]

IN THE COURSE of developing emotional responsibility, most of us experience three stages: (1) "emotional slavery"—believing ourselves responsible for the feelings of others, (2) "the obnoxious stage"—in which we refuse to admit to caring what anyone else feels or needs, and (3) "emotional liberation"—in which we accept full responsibility for our own feelings but not the feelings of others, while being aware that we can never meet our own needs at the expense of others. [5]

〜

WE DENY RESPONSIBILITY for our actions when we attribute their cause to factors outside ourselves:

Vague, impersonal forces—*"I cleaned my room because I had to."*

Our condition, diagnosis, or personal or psychological history—*"I drink because I am an alcoholic."*

The actions of others—*"I hit my child because he ran into the street."*

The dictates of authority—*"I lied to the client because the boss told me to."*

Group pressure—*"I started smoking because all my friends did."*

Institutional policies, rules, and regulations—*"I have to suspend you for this infraction because it's the school policy."*

Gender roles, social roles, or age roles—*"I hate going to work, but I do it because I am a husband and a father."*

Uncontrollable impulses—*"I was overcome by my urge to eat the candy bar."* [5]

〜

IF YOU WANT to break peace, deny responsibility for your actions. [29]

20

SHARING OUR APPRECIATION AND GRATITUDE

APPRECIATION

SEE, IT'S JUST as important for me that people hear my appreciation as my messages of distress. I want to make sure they hear them both, and not hear my pain as a criticism and not hear my appreciation as a compliment or as praise. [10]

◡

THE THREE THINGS we need to express appreciation—not praise, because there is no such thing as praise in NVC. Praise is a classical judging technique; managers love it because they say research shows that employees perform better if you praise them at least once a day. That does work for a while until the employees see the manipulation in it. We never give appreciation in NVC to try to create some result in the other person. We only give it to celebrate, to let the other person know how great we feel about something that they have done. The three things are:

1. What the other person has done that we appreciate, and we are very specific about that,

2. Our feelings, and

3. Our needs that have been fulfilled. [1]

ᔆ

WHEN WE USE NVC to express appreciation, it is purely to celebrate, not to get something in return. Our sole intention is to celebrate the way our lives have been enriched by others. [5]

ᔆ

CONVENTIONAL COMPLIMENTS OFTEN take the form of judgments however positive, and are sometimes offered to manipulate the behavior of others. NVC encourages the expression of appreciation solely for celebration. [34]

ᔆ

FOR MANY OF us, it is difficult to receive appreciation gracefully. We fret over whether we deserve it. We worry about what's being expected of us—especially if we have teachers or managers who use appreciation as a means to spur productivity. Or we're nervous about living up to the appreciation. Accustomed to a culture where buying, earning, and deserving are the standard modes of interchange, we are often uncomfortable with simple giving and receiving.

NVC encourages us to receive appreciation with the same quality of empathy we express when listening to other messages. We hear what we have done that has contributed to others' well-being; we hear their feelings and the needs that were fulfilled. We take into our hearts the joyous reality that we can each enhance the quality of others' lives. [5]

ᔆ

I FIND IT tragic that we work so hard to buy love and assume that we must deny ourselves and do for others in order to be liked. In fact, when we do things solely in the spirit of enhancing life, we will find others appreciating us.[5]

GRATITUDE

IT'S EXTREMELY IMPORTANT that we build into our lives opportunities to exchange sincere gratitude, that we have opportunities to express it to others and to receive it.[31]

⤳

IN MIDDLE CLASS culture the need is for gratitude. Recognition. And people are so brought up to believe that you shouldn't have that need, you should just give out of selflessness and so forth, that they're ashamed to admit that they have a need to celebrate what they did, to have some recognition for it. So they go out and bore people with all the stories, not realizing that's going to get the exact opposite of what they want.[20]

⤳

THE MORE GRATITUDE is a part of our life . . . the more fuel we have to be a giraffe in a jackal-speaking world.[22]

⤳

SO THERE IS a severe fuel shortage on this planet. It's amazing how many people are gratitude-starved. They're not getting the gratitude necessary to know that we have met our needs to enrich life. And if we're not getting that gratitude back, regularly, to confirm that that need is being met, the cost of not having our need for meaning met is enormous. It just takes the joy out of life. Takes the energy out of life.[17]

⤳

SO WE NEED to be, above all, very clear that we not mix up gratitude as a need. We don't need gratitude. If we think we need gratitude, then we're suckers to live our life trying to get approval from others. Gratitude is very important, but not as a need. It's necessary as a confirmation that our need was met. [17]

‍↬

NOW, IT'S NOT enough that we do things out of an intention to enrich life, we have to have a feedback mechanism. And gratitude is that feedback mechanism. But unfortunately the domination world, seeing the power of this, has learned to turn this natural function into an oppression by getting people addicted to rewards. It distorts the need to enrich life. [17]

‍↬

SO, THE FIRST thing that I would suggest, then, in the giving of gratitude to other people, is to be very careful that you never give gratitude as a reward. Never give gratitude to build up someone's confidence in themself. In other words, don't use it as a manipulation to create something in the other person. [17]

‍↬

THE INTENT IS very important in giving gratitude. It must be only to celebrate life. To celebrate a need of ours getting met. Absolutely no intent to reward the other person, just coming from the heart. [27]

‍↬

IT'S VERY HARD for people who don't use NVC to hear gratitude expressed from the heart. Why? Because they've been living in a world that hears gratitude as a judgment. They wonder whether they deserved it or they wonder whether it's being used as a reward, because very often "thank you" is used as a reward, which is a sure way to spoil the beauty of gratitude. [10]

IF WE DON'T know how to deal with our pain, then the gratitude cannot come sincerely. And a lot of people don't know how to deal with the pain, so the gratitude gets smothered behind the pain. [17]

GRATITUDE IS ANOTHER vital part of social change, but it's also important in helping to sustain a kind of spiritual consciousness that Nonviolent Communication tries to support. When we know how to express and receive gratitude in a certain way, it gives us enormous energy to sustain our social-change efforts, as well as to sustain us through the beauty of what can be, rather than attempting to conquer evil forces. [8]

GRATITUDE ALSO PLAYS a big role for me. If I am conscious of a human act that I want to express gratitude for, conscious of how I feel when the act occurs, whether it's my act or someone else's, and what needs of mine it fulfills, then expressing gratitude fills me with consciousness of the power that we human beings have to enrich lives. It makes me aware that we are divine energy, that we have such power to make life wonderful, and that there is nothing we like better than to do just that. [6]

TO EXPRESS A celebration, a gratitude in giraffe: clear observation, present feeling, and a fulfilled need. Those are the three things to get across. [17]

HOW DO WE express gratitude in Nonviolent Communication? First, the intent is all-important: to celebrate life, nothing else. We're not trying to reward the other person. We want the other person to know how our life has been enriched by what they did. That's our only intent. To make clear how our life has been enriched, we need to say three things to people, and praise and compliments don't make these three things clear:

1. We want to make clear what the person did that we want to celebrate, what action on their part enriched our lives.

2. We want to tell them how we feel about that, what feelings are alive in us as a result of what they've done.

3. We want to tell them what needs of ours were met by their actions. [8]

⤳

WE FIND IN every country how hard it is for people to receive gratitude, because their prior training has taught them that you should be humble, you shouldn't think you're anything. [8]

⤳

IT MAKES IT hard even to receive gratitude when you have to worry about whether or not you earned it. [8]

21

DAILY PRACTICES

TO PRACTICE NVC, we must completely abandon the goal of getting other people to do what we want. [34]

⤺

EVERY TIME I mess up is a chance to practice. [34]

⤺

I KEEP A jackal book. A jackal book is just something to write on that I want to have handy at all times, so anytime I see myself getting disconnected and doing or living in a way that is not in harmony with how I choose to be, I'll make a note of it, so I can learn from this. You see? So that's one thing I can do. I can learn when I lose it. [12]

⤺

HOWEVER IMPRESSED WE may be with NVC concepts, it is only through practice and application that our lives are transformed. [34]

⤺

ONE OF THE best messages I ever heard any of my teachers say, [was from] Carl Rogers, the psychologist. [He] said, "If you're alive, you'll always be a little bit frightened." So, if you're really secure and you know what's right, poor you. You've died and you don't even know it. [17]

⤳

DON'T HATE THE circumstance, you may miss the blessing. [34]

⤳

I BELIEVE EVERYONE has a right to dance and sing even if they move and sound like a crow with a crippled wing. [35]

⤳

I CERTAINLY LIKE the change I see in myself, now, from when I started. But there are still times when it is very difficult for me to connect with other people in a way that I choose to. And when I don't, it's very helpful if I make a note of it. I like to keep a jackal book handy—I call it my jackal book. So whenever I respond in a way that really is not in harmony with how I choose to [live], I want to learn from it. [26]

⤳

I KEEP A giraffe book for celebrating life. For reminding myself every morning of something I've done in the last twenty-four hours that enriched life for somebody—myself, others, or both. The more I remind myself of that—why would I do anything else throughout the day? The more I remind myself, also, of what others have done to enrich my life, the more I keep that focus that we each have that power to enrich life, every moment of every day. [12]

⤳

> **Don't hate the circumstance,
> you may miss the
> blessing.** [34]

PARTICIPANT. **MARSHALL, I WOULD** also like you to mention the three things that it takes to become proficient at NVC.

MARSHALL. First of all, the good news is that it doesn't require us to be perfect. It does not require us to be saints. And we don't have to be patient. We don't have to have positive self-esteem; we don't have to have self-confidence. I have demonstrated that you don't even have to be a normal person. [*Laughter*]

What does it take? First and foremost, spiritual clarity. We have to be highly conscious how we want to connect with human beings. We're living in a society, I'm afraid to say, that is largely judgmental in its history and evolution. It's leaning toward NVC, very rapidly, if you listen to Teilhard Chardin. He was a paleontologist who thinks in terms of tens of thousands of years. But it's not moving as fast as I'd like, so I'm doing what I can to speed it up. The main thing I'm trying to do is work on myself. When I get myself fully engaged with NVC, I think I am helping the planet; then what energy I have left over, I use to try to help other people become engaged with NVC. So the most important thing is spiritual clarity, that we be highly conscious of how we want to connect with people. For me, I have to stop every day—two, three, four times—really stop, and remind myself how I want to connect with other people in this world.

How do I do that? This is individual for everyone. Some people call it meditation, prayer, stopping and slowing down, whatever you call it. I do it differently every day myself, but it's basically just stopping and slowing down and doing a check on what is running through my head. Are judgments running through my head? Is NVC running through my head? I stop and look at what is going on in there and slow down. I remind myself of the "subtle sneaky important reason why I was born a human being and not a chair," to use a line from one of my favorite plays, *A Thousand Clowns*. So that's the most important thing: spiritual clarity.

Second: practice, practice, practice. I make a note every time I catch myself judging myself or other people. I make a note of what was the stimulus for this. What did I do? What did others say or do that, all of a sudden, I gave myself permission to turn back into judgment? Then I use that. Sometime in the day I sit and look at my list, and I try to give myself empathy for the pain that was going on in me at the time. I try not to beat myself up. I try to hear what pain was going on in me that led me to speak in that way. Then I ask myself: "How could I have used NVC in that situation? What might the other person have been feeling and needing?" Now, NVC-ers love to mess things up because an NVC-er doesn't try to be perfect. We know the danger of trying to be perfect. We just try to become progressively less stupid. . . . When your objective is to become progressively less stupid, every time you mess something up, it becomes cause for a celebration. It gives you a chance to learn how to be less stupid. So practice, practice, practice learning how to be less stupid.

And third, it really helps to be part of an NVC support community. We are living in a judgmental world and it helps to create an NVC world around us from which we can now start to build a greater world, an NVC world. That is why I am so grateful that we have all of the NVC teams locally.[1]

THE GOAL OF life is not to be perfect, it's to become progressively less stupid.[19]

PLAY

I TRY TO never do anything I should do, but follow Joseph Campbell's suggestion. After studying comparative religion and mythology for forty-three years, Campbell said, "You know, after all of my research, it's amazing that all religions are saying the same thing: Don't do anything that isn't playful."

Don't do anything that isn't play. He says it another way: "Follow your bliss," come from this energy of how to make the world fun and learnable.[2]

ALMOST ALL OF the religions and mythologies I've studied say a very similar message, one that Joseph Campbell, the mythologist, summarizes in some of his work: *Don't do anything that isn't play.* And what they mean by *play* is willingly contributing to life. So, don't do anything to avoid punishment; don't do anything for rewards; don't do anything out of guilt, shame, and the vicious concepts of duty and obligation. What you do will be play when you can see how it enriches life. [6]

↩

DON'T DO ANYTHING that isn't play. And it'll be play if you choose to do it, seeing how it's going to enrich life. [26]

↩

WHAT ALL THE basic religions are saying is this: Don't do anything that isn't play. [34]

TOLERANCE

LET'S TALK FOR a minute about "tolerance." There are a lot of people that I can't stand being around. And they are my best gurus. They teach me about what's going on in me that makes it hard to see the divine energy in them. I want to learn from anything that keeps me from connecting to that energy. Fortunately, there are a lot of people I can't stand; I have a lot of learning opportunities. I practice. I ask, "What does this person do that is a trigger for my judging them?" First I try to get clear about what they do, and second, conscious about how I'm judging that person who makes me so angry. The third step is to look behind my judgment to see what particular need of mine is not getting met in relation to that person. I try to give myself empathy for what need of mine isn't met in relation to that person. Fourth, I say to myself,

"When the person does that thing that I don't like, what personal need are they trying to meet?" I try to empathize with what's alive in them when they do it. [2]

TAKE YOUR TIME

TO PRACTICE NVC, it's critical for me to be able to slow down, take my time, to come from an energy I choose, the one I believe that we were meant to come from, not the one I was programmed into. I start the day with a remembering of where I want to be. [34]

⤳

NONVIOLENT COMMUNICATION REQUIRES that we take our time to come from our divine energy rather than our cultural programming. [8]

⤳

IN THE MIDDLE of the rat race it's very important for me to know how to choose to make use of the three words I probably said to myself more than any three words in the last forty years: "TAKE YOUR TIME." Those three words give you the power to come from a spirituality of your own choosing, not the one you were programmed for. [2]

⤳

I CARRY WITH me a picture of a son of a friend of mine. It was the last picture taken before he was killed in the battle of Lebanon. The reason I keep this picture with me is that, in the last picture, the son was wearing a T-shirt and the T-shirt said Take Your Time. And that's a very powerful symbol to me. It's probably the most important part for me in learning this process, learning how to live by it. Take your time. Yes, it feels awkward at times not to behave out of the

> I know whenever I'm angry,
> guilty, depressed, or ashamed,
> I'm not alive. [22]

automatic way I was trained, but I want to take my time so that I live my life in harmony with my own values instead of in a robot-like way, automatically carrying out the way I was programmed by the culture in which I was raised. So, yes, take your time. It may feel awkward, but for me it's my life. I'm going to take my time to live it in a way I want. I can look silly with that perhaps. [9]

〜

IN MY MEDITATION materials, I have a very powerful picture that helps me remember to take my time. A friend of mine from Israel is very active organizing Israelis and Palestinians who've lost children in the struggle, and who want to create something else out of the misery. So, one of the steps was to write a book in honor of his son who was killed. . . . I opened it up and there on the first page is the last picture taken of his son before he was killed in the battle of Lebanon. On the son's T-shirt it says, Take Your Time.

I asked my friend, the author father, if he had a bigger-sized picture that I could have to help me remember. I told him why those three words were so important to me. He said: "Then let me tell you also, Marshall, this will probably make it even more powerful. When I went to my son's commanding officer to ask, 'Why did you send him? Couldn't you see that anybody you asked to do that was going to get killed?' he said, 'We didn't take our time.' That's why I put that picture in there of my son." [2]

〜

I KNOW WHENEVER I'm angry, guilty, depressed, or ashamed, I'm not alive. I'm up in my head jackaling people: myself, or others. I'm not alive, I'm not really connected to my needs or theirs. If I react out of that energy, I've never gotten my needs met. So, take my time, take my time. Come back to life before I open my mouth. [22]

〜

TAKE YOUR TIME to understand. Don't just do something, be there. [34]

⌇

I RECALL ONE time when I was first learning NVC, my older son and I were having a conflict. My first reaction to what he was saying was not to connect with what was alive in him, with what he was feeling and needing. I wanted to jump in and show him he was wrong. I had to take a deep, deep breath. I needed to see what was going on in me for a moment and see that I was losing connection with him, then bring my attention back to him, saying, "So, you're feeling . . ." and "you're needing . . ." to try to connect with him.

Then he said something else, and again I got triggered and had to slow down and take a deep breath to be able to keep coming back to what was alive in him. Of course, all this was taking longer than usual in the conversation up to that point, and he had some friends waiting for him outside.

Finally, he said, "Daddy, it's taking you so long to talk."

I said, "Let me tell you what I can say quickly. Do it my way, or I'll kick your butt."

He said, "Take your time, Dad, take your time."

So, Nonviolent Communication requires that we take our time to come from our divine energy rather than our cultural programming. [8]

WORKS CITED

This list references the superscript number after each quote.

Books

1. Rosenberg, Marshall B. *Being Me, Loving You: A Practical Guide to Extraordinary Relationships.* Encinitas, CA: PuddleDancer Press, 2005.

2. Rosenberg, Marshall B. *Getting Past the Pain Between Us: Healing and Reconciliation Without Compromise.* Encinitas, CA: PuddleDancer Press, 2005.

3. Rosenberg, Marshall B. *The Heart of Social Change: How You Can Make a Difference in Your World.* Encinitas, CA: PuddleDancer Press, 2005.

4. Rosenberg, Marshall B. *Life-Enriching Education: Nonviolent Communication Helps Schools Improve Performance, Reduce Conflict, and Enhance Relationships.* Encinitas, CA: PuddleDancer Press, 2003.

5. Rosenberg, Marshall B. *Nonviolent Communication: A Language of Life.* 3rd ed. Encinitas, CA: PuddleDancer Press, 2015.

6. Rosenberg, Marshall B. *Practical Spirituality: Reflections on the Spiritual Basis of Nonviolent Communication.* Encinitas, CA: PuddleDancer Press, 2004.

7. Rosenberg, Marshall B. *Raising Children Compassionately: Parenting the Nonviolent Communication Way.* Encinitas, CA: PuddleDancer Press, 2005.

8. Rosenberg, Marshall B. *Speak Peace in a World of Conflict: What You Say Next Will Change Your World.* Encinitas, CA: PuddleDancer Press, 2005.

9. Rosenberg, Marshall B. *The Surprising Purpose of Anger: Beyond Anger Management: Finding the Gift.* Encinitas, CA: PuddleDancer Press, 2005.

10. Rosenberg, Marshall B. *Teaching Children Compassionately: How Students and Teachers Can Succeed With Mutual Understanding.* Encinitas, CA: PuddleDancer Press, 2005.

11. Rosenberg, Marshall B. *We Can Work It Out: Resolving Conflicts Peacefully and Powerfully.* Encinitas, CA: PuddleDancer Press, 2005.

Workshops

12. Rosenberg, Marshall B. "Basics of Nonviolent Communication." Workshop. Oregon Network for Compassionate Communication, n.d.

13. Rosenberg, Marshall B. "Bonding and Healing." Workshop. n.d.

14. Rosenberg, Marshall B. "Compassionate Communication." Workshop. San Diego, n.d.

15. Rosenberg, Marshall B. "Creating a Life-Serving System Within Oneself." Workshop. Corona 2000 Recording Series. Corona, CA, November 2000.

16. Rosenberg, Marshall B. "Experiencing Needs as a Gift." Workshop. Corona 2000 Recording Series. Corona, CA, November 2000.

17. Rosenberg, Marshall B. "Giraffe Fuel." Workshop. Corona 2000 Recording Series. Corona, CA, November 2000.

18. Rosenberg, Marshall B. "Healing and Reconciliation." Workshop. October 2002.

19. Rosenberg, Marshall B. "Healing Emotional Pain." Workshop. Bay Area Nonviolent Communication, n.d.

20. Rosenberg, Marshall B. "Intimate Relationships." Workshop. Corona 2000 Recording Series. Corona, CA, November 2000.

21. Rosenberg, Marshall B. "Introduction to Nonviolent Communication." Workshop. Bay Area Nonviolent Communication, n.d.

22. Rosenberg, Marshall B. "Making Life Wonderful: An Intermediate Training in Nonviolent Communication." Workshop. n.d.

23. Rosenberg, Marshall B. "Marriage in the 90s." Workshop. n.d.

24. Rosenberg, Marshall B. "MBR Story on Healing From Rape." Workshop. n.d.

25. Rosenberg, Marshall B. "Needs and Empathy." Workshop. Corona 2000 Recording Series, Corona, CA. November 2000.

26. Rosenberg, Marshall B. "NVC Basics Daylong." Workshop. n.d.

27. Rosenberg, Marshall B. "NVC in Business." Workshop. October 2002.

28. Rosenberg, Marshall B. "Overcoming Prejudice." Workshop. Bay Area Nonviolent Communication, n.d.

29. Rosenberg, Marshall B. "Power to Create World." Workshop. n.d.

30. Rosenberg, Marshall B. "Reconciliation and Forgiveness." Workshop. n.d.

Websites

31. Danforth, David. (@MBR_Quotes) November 2021–August 2022. Twitter account. https://twitter.com/MBR_Quotes/status/1508586281197924355.

32. Rosenberg, Marshall B. Excerpted from "Marshall Rosenberg: The Dynamics of Empathy." YouTube Channel Michael Hurin, August 19, 2019. Recorded radio broadcast. WGDR Plainfield, VT, Community Radio from Goddard College, n.d. 1 hr., 30 min. https://www.youtube.com/watch?v=tahOuqFS8kM&t=0s.

33. Rosenberg, Marshall B. "How to Apologize in Giraffe." Audio recording. YouTube Channel Giraffe NVC, December 1, 2020. https://www.youtube.com/watch?v=23io32hFv-Q. Excerpted from "The Basics of Nonviolent Communication, with Marshall B. Rosenberg, PhD." YouTube Channel Nadania Centrum, October 27, 2015. Audio recording of workshop. 3 hr. San Francisco. April 2000. https://www.youtube.com/watch?v=l7TONauJGfc&t=0s.

34. Rosenberg, Marshall B. "Marshall Rosenberg Quotes." Nonviolent Communication Books & Resources. Free Resources. PuddleDancer Press. Website. https://www.nonviolentcommunication.com/resources/mbr-quotes/.

35. Rosenberg, Marshall B. Song "A Crow with a Crippled Wing" at 1:56, Excerpted from "Marshall Rosenberg Nonviolent Communication Resolving CConflicts [sic]." YouTube Channel Michael Hurin, August 4, 2019. Audio recording of workshop, "Resolving Conflicts with Children." 2.5 hr. Cuyahoga Community College, Cleveland, OH. November 21, 1991. https://www.youtube.com/watch?v=8kaVztNodEM.

LIST OF MAJOR NVC
TERMS AND NVC THEMES

The Four-Part Nonviolent Communication Process

Clearly expressing how **I am** without blaming or criticizing	Empathically receiving how **you are** without hearing blame or criticism

OBSERVATIONS

1. What I observe *(see, hear, remember, imagine, free from my evaluations)* that does or does not contribute to my well-being: *"When I (see, hear) . . . "*	1. What you observe *(see, hear, remember, imagine, free from your evaluations)* that does or does not contribute to your well-being: *"When you see/hear . . . "* <small>*(Sometimes unspoken when offering empathy)*</small>

FEELINGS

2. How I feel *(emotion or sensation rather than thought)* in relation to what I observe: *"I feel . . . "*	2. How you feel *(emotion or sensation rather than thought)* in relation to what you observe: *"You feel . . ."*

NEEDS

3. What I need or value *(rather than a preference, or a specific action)* that causes my feelings: *" . . . because I need/value . . . "*	3. What you need or value *(rather than a preference, or a specific action)* that causes your feelings: *" . . . because you need/value . . ."*

Clearly requesting that which would enrich **my** life without demanding	Empathically receiving that which would enrich **your** life without hearing any demand

REQUESTS

4. The concrete actions I would like taken: *"Would you be willing to . . . ?"*	4. The concrete actions you would like taken: *"Would you like . . . ?"* <small>*(Sometimes unspoken when offering empathy)*</small>

© Marshall B. Rosenberg. For more information about Marshall B. Rosenberg
or the Center for Nonviolent Communication, please visit www.CNVC.org.

Some Basic Feelings We All Have

Feelings when needs are fulfilled

- Amazed
- Comfortable
- Confident
- Eager
- Energetic
- Fulfilled
- Glad
- Hopeful
- Inspired
- Intrigued
- Joyous
- Moved
- Optimistic
- Proud
- Relieved
- Stimulated
- Surprised
- Thankful
- Touched
- Trustful

Feelings when needs are not fulfilled

- Angry
- Annoyed
- Concerned
- Confused
- Disappointed
- Discouraged
- Distressed
- Embarrassed
- Frustrated
- Helpless
- Hopeless
- Impatient
- Irritated
- Lonely
- Nervous
- Overwhelmed
- Puzzled
- Reluctant
- Sad
- Uncomfortable

 # Some Basic Needs We All Have

Autonomy
- Choosing dreams/goals/values
- Choosing plans for fulfilling one's dreams, goals, values

Celebration
- Celebrating the creation of life and dreams fulfilled
- Celebrating losses: loved ones, dreams, etc. (mourning)

Integrity
- Authenticity • Creativity
- Meaning • Self-worth

Interdependence
- Acceptance • Appreciation
- Closeness • Community
- Consideration
- Contribution to the enrichment of life
- Emotional Safety • Empathy

Physical Nurturance
- Air • Food
- Movement, exercise
- Protection from life-threatening forms of life: viruses, bacteria, insects, predatory animals
- Rest • Sexual Expression
- Shelter • Touch • Water

Play
- Fun • Laughter

Spiritual Communion
- Beauty • Harmony
- Inspiration • Order • Peace

- Honesty (the empowering honesty that enables us to learn from our limitations)
- Love • Reassurance
- Respect • Support
- Trust • Understanding

Nonviolent Communication Summary of Basic Concepts

NONVIOLENT/LIFE-CONNECTED COMMUNICATION	LIFE-ALIENATED COMMUNICATION
Power WITH others	Power OVER others
Win/win (I/thou)	Win/lose or lose/lose (you or I)
Process language	Static language
Focus on HOW people are (how they feel and what they need)	Focus on WHAT people are (labels, diagnoses, interpretations)
Value judgments	Moralistic judgments
Requests	Demands
PURPOSE: to create and maintain a certain quality of connection to allow everyone to get their needs met	PURPOSE: to get what we want
Inspires compassionate response	Tends to produce aggressive or indifferent response
Force used only to protect life	Force used punitively
Acceptance of choice and responsibility for one's actions and feelings originating from one's met or unmet needs	Denial of choice and responsibility for one's feelings, originating from actions by others or situations outside of oneself
No blame of self or others	Blame of self and/or others
Motivation based on seeing how one's actions contribute to life, meeting needs of self and others (intrinsic motivation)	Motivation based on guilt, shame, fear of punishment, hope for reward (extrinsic motivation)
Interdependence AND autonomy	Dependence/independence

© Gary Baran and Center for Nonviolent Communication.

Differentiating Between Feelings and Faux Feelings

This list includes suggestions for use in translating words often confused with feelings. For example, when someone says "I'm feeling *rejected*," you might translate as "Are you feeling *scared* because you have a need for *inclusion*?"

FAUX FEELINGS	FEELINGS	NEEDS
Abandoned	Terrified, hurt, bewildered, sad, frightened, lonely	Nurturing, connection, belonging, support, caring
Abused	Angry, frustrated, frightened	Caring, nurturing, support, emotional or physical well-being, consideration
(Not) accepted	Upset, scared, lonely	Inclusion, connection, community, belonging, contribution, peer respect
Attacked	Scared, angry	Safety
Belittled	Angry, frustrated, tense, distressed	Respect, autonomy, to be seen, acknowledgment, appreciation
Betrayed	Angry, hurt, disappointed, enraged	Trust, dependability, honesty, honor, commitment, clarity
Blamed	Angry, scared, confused, antagonistic, hostile, hurt	Accountability, causality, fairness, justice
Bullied	Angry, scared, pressured	Autonomy, choice, safety
Caged/boxed in	Angry, thwarted, scared	Autonomy, choice, freedom
Cancelled	Angry, hurt, fearful	Understanding, acceptance, care
Cheated	Resentful, hurt, angry	Honesty, fairness, justice, trust
Coerced	Angry, frustrated, scared, frightened, thwarted	Choice, autonomy, freedom, act freely, choose freely
Cornered	Angry, scared, anxious	Autonomy, freedom
Criticized	In pain, scared, angry anxious, humiliated	Understanding, acknowledgment, accountability, nonjudgmental
Discounted/ diminished	Hurt, angry, embarrassed, frustrated	Need to matter, acknowledgment, inclusion, recognition, respect
Disliked	Sad, lonely, hurt	Connection, appreciation, friendship
Distrusted	Sad, frustrated	Trust, honesty
Dumped on	Angry, overwhelmed	Respect, consideration
Harassed	Angry, frustrated, scared	Respect, space, consideration, peace
Hassled	Irritated, distressed, angry	Serenity, autonomy, calm
Ignored	Lonely, scared, hurt, sad	Connection, belonging, inclusion
Insulted	Angry, embarrassed	Respect, consideration, recognition
Interrupted	Angry, frustrated, hurt	Respect, to be heard, consideration
Intimidated	Scared, anxious	Safety, equality, empowerment
Invalidated	Angry, hurt, resentful	Appreciation, respect, recognition

© John Kinyon, CNVC mediator and trainer, cocreator of the Mediate Your Life approach to conflict.

FAUX FEELINGS	FEELINGS	NEEDS
Invisible	Sad, angry, lonely, scared	Seen and heard, inclusion, belonging
Isolated	Lonely, afraid, scared	Community, inclusion, belonging
Left out	Sad, lonely, anxious	Inclusion, belonging, connection
Let down	Sad, disappointed, scared	Consistency, trust, dependability
Manipulated	Angry, scared, powerless, thwarted, frustrated	Autonomy, empowerment, trust, equality, freedom, free choice
Mistrusted	Sad, angry	Trust
Misunderstood	Upset, angry, frustrated	To be heard, understanding, clarity
Neglected	Lonely, scared	Connection, inclusion, participation
Overpowered	Angry, impotent, helpless	Equality, justice, autonomy, freedom
Overworked	Angry, tired, frustrated	Respect, consideration, rest, caring
Patronized	Angry, frustrated, resentful	Recognition, equality, respect
Pressured	Anxious, resentful	Relaxation, clarity, consideration
Provoked	Angry, frustrated, hostile	Respect, consideration
Put down	Angry, sad, embarrassed	Respect, understanding
Rejected	Hurt, scared, angry, defiant	Belonging, inclusion, connection
Ripped off/ screwed	Anger, resentment, disappointment	Consideration, justice, fairness, acknowledgment, trust
Smothered/ suffocated	Frustrated, fear, desperation	Space, freedom, autonomy, authenticity, self-expression
Taken for granted	Sad, angry, hurt, disappointment	Appreciation, acknowledgment, recognition, consideration
Threatened	Scared, alarmed, agitated	Safety, autonomy
Trampled	Angry, frustrated, overwhelmed	Empowerment, connection, equality, community, consideration, respect
Tricked	Embarrassed, resentful	Integrity, trust, honesty
Unappreciated	Sad, angry, hurt, frustrated	Appreciation, respect, consideration
Unheard	Sad, hostile, frustrated	Understanding, consideration
Unloved	Sad, bewildered, frustrated	Love, appreciation, connection
Unseen	Sad, anxious, frustrated	Acknowledgment, appreciation
Unsupported	Sad, hurt, resentful	Support, understanding
Unwanted	Sad, anxious, frustrated	Belonging, inclusion, caring
Used	Sad, angry, resentful	Autonomy, equality, consideration
Victimized	Frightened, helpless	Empowerment, safety, justice
Violated	Sad, agitated, anxious	Privacy, safety, trust, space, respect
Wronged	Angry, hurt, resentful	Respect, justice, trust, safety, fairness

© John Kinyon, CNVC mediator and trainer, cocreator of the Mediate Your Life approach to conflict.

Nonviolent Communication Research

You can find an up-to-date list of journal articles, dissertations, theses, project reports, and independent studies exploring various facets of Nonviolent Communication at: www.nonviolentcommunication.com/ learn-nonviolent-communication/research-on-nvc/

Some of these are qualitative, some quantitative, and some are mixed methods. Together they begin to offer an evidence base. If you have completed NVC research and would like to add your paper to the list, please contact us at: www.nonviolentcommunication.com/feedback-form/

About Nonviolent Communication

Nonviolent Communication has flourished for more than four decades across sixty countries selling more than 6,000,000 books in over thirty-five languages for one simple reason: it works.

Nonviolent Communication is changing lives every day. NVC provides an easy-to-grasp, effective method to get to the root of violence and pain peacefully. By examining the unmet needs behind what we do and say, NVC helps reduce hostility, heal pain, and strengthen professional and personal relationships. NVC is being taught in corporations, classrooms, prisons, and mediation centers worldwide. And it is affecting cultural shifts as institutions, corporations, and governments integrate NVC consciousness into their organizational structures and their approach to leadership.

Most of us want the skills to improve the quality of our relationships, to deepen our sense of personal empowerment, or simply to help us communicate more effectively. Unfortunately, most of us are educated from birth to compete, judge, demand, and diagnose; to think and communicate in terms of what is "right" and "wrong" with people. At best, the habitual ways we think and speak hinder communication and create misunderstanding or frustration. And still worse, they can cause anger and pain, and may lead to violence. Without wanting to, even people with the best of intentions generate needless conflict.

NVC helps us reach beneath the surface and discover what is alive and vital within us, and how all of our actions are based on human needs that we are seeking to meet. We learn to develop a vocabulary of feelings and needs that helps us more clearly express what is going on in us at any given moment. When we understand and acknowledge our needs, we develop a shared foundation for much more satisfying relationships. Join the thousands of people worldwide who have improved their relationships and their lives with this simple yet revolutionary process.

About PuddleDancer Press

Visit the PDP website at www.NonviolentCommunication.com. We have a resource-rich and ever-growing website that currently addresses 50+ topics related to NVC through articles, online resources, handouts, Marshall Rosenberg quotes, and so much more. Please come visit us.

- **NVC Quick Connect e-Newsletter**—Sign up online to receive our monthly e-Newsletter, filled with expert articles on timely and relevant topics, links to NVC in the news, inspirational and fun quotes and songs, announcements of trainings and other NVC events, and exclusive specials on NVC learning materials.
- **Shop NVC**—Purchase our NVC titles safely, affordably, and conveniently online. Find everyday discounts on individual titles, multiple copies, and book packages. Learn more about our authors and read endorsements of NVC from world-renowned communication experts and peacemakers.
- **About NVC**—Learn more about the unique life-changing communication and conflict resolution skills of NVC (also known as Compassionate Communication, Collaborative Communication, Respectful Communication, Mindful Communication, Peaceful Communication, or Effective Communication). Find an overview of the NVC process, key facts about NVC, and more.
- **About Marshall Rosenberg**—Read about the world-renowned peacemaker, educator, best-selling author, and founder of the Center for Nonviolent Communication, including press materials, a biography, and more.

For more information, please contact PuddleDancer Press at:

2240 Encinitas Blvd., Ste. D-911 • Encinitas, CA 92024
Phone: 760-557-0326 • Email: email@puddledancer.com
www.NonviolentCommunication.com

About the Center for Nonviolent Communication

The Center for Nonviolent Communication (CNVC) is an international nonprofit peacemaking organization whose vision is a world where everyone's needs are met peacefully. CNVC is devoted to supporting the spread of Nonviolent Communication (NVC) around the world.

Founded in 1984 by Dr. Marshall B. Rosenberg, CNVC has been contributing to a vast social transformation in thinking, speaking and acting—showing people how to connect in ways that inspire compassionate results. NVC is now being taught around the globe in communities, schools, prisons, mediation centers, churches, businesses, professional conferences, and more. Hundreds of certified trainers and hundreds more supporters teach NVC to tens of thousands of people each year in more than sixty countries.

CNVC believes that NVC training is a crucial step to continue building a compassionate, peaceful society. Your tax-deductible donation will help CNVC continue to provide training in some of the most impoverished, violent corners of the world. It will also support the development and continuation of organized projects aimed at bringing NVC training to high-need geographic regions and populations.

To make a tax-deductible donation or to learn more about the valuable resources described below, visit the CNVC website at www. CNVC.org:

- **Training and Certification**—Find local, national, and international training opportunities, access trainer certification information, connect to local NVC communities, trainers, and more.

- **CNVC Bookstore**—Find mail or phone order information for a complete selection of NVC books, booklets, audio, and video materials at the CNVC website.

- **CNVC Projects**—Participate in one of the several regional and theme-based projects that provide focus and leadership for teaching NVC in a particular application or geographic region.

For more information, please contact CNVC at:
US Only: 800-255-7696 • Email: cnvc@CNVC.org • Website: www.CNVC.org

Nonviolent Communication,

3rd Edition

A Language of Life

By Marshall B. Rosenberg, PhD

$19.95 – Trade Paper 6x9, 264pp
ISBN: 978-1-892005-28-1

What is Violent Communication?

If "violent" means acting in ways that result in hurt or harm, then much of how we communicate —judging others, bullying, having racial bias, blaming, finger pointing, discriminating, speaking without listening, criticizing others or ourselves, name-calling, reacting when angry, using political rhetoric, being defensive or judging who's "good/bad" or what's "right/wrong" with people—**could indeed be called "violent communication."**

What is Nonviolent Communication?

Nonviolent Communication is the integration of four things:

- Consciousness: a set of principles that support living a life of compassion, collaboration, courage, and authenticity

- Language: understanding how words contribute to connection or distance

- Communication: knowing how to ask for what we want, how to hear others even in disagreement, and how to move toward solutions that work for all

- Means of influence: sharing "power with others" rather than using "power over others"

Nonviolent Communication Toolkit for Facilitators

Interactive Activities and Awareness Exercises Based on 18 Key Concepts for the Development of NVC Skills and Consciousness

By Judi Morin, Raj Gill, and Lucy Leu

$29.95 — Trade Paper 7x10, 400pp
ISBN: 978-1-934336-45-8

Develop NVC Skills and Consciousness!

Internationally respected NVC trainers, Judi Morin, Raj Gill, and Lucy Leu have come together to codify more than twenty years of training experience in one hands-on facilitator guide. Whether you're a new facilitator, a seasoned trainer looking to incorporate a more experiential approach, or a team of trainers, the *Nonviolent Communication Toolkit for Facilitators* has a wealth of resources for you. By breaking Nonviolent Communication down into 18 key concepts, this toolkit provides succinct teaching tools that can be used on their own for shorter sessions, or combined for a long-term or multi-session training.

Nonviolent Communication Companion Workbook, 2nd Edition

A Practical Guide for Individual, Group, or Classroom Study

By Lucy Leu

$21.95 — Trade Paper 7x10, 240pp
ISBN: 978-1-892005-29-8

Putting NVC Skills Into Practice!

Learning Nonviolent Communication has often been equated with learning a whole new language. *The NVC Companion Workbook* helps you put these powerful, effective skills into practice with chapter-by-chapter study of Marshall Rosenberg's cornerstone text, *NVC: A Language of Life*. Create a safe, supportive group learning or practice environment that nurtures the needs of each participant. Find a wealth of activities, exercises, and facilitator suggestions to refine and practice this powerful communication process.

Nonviolent Communication has flourished for more than four decades across sixty countries selling more than 6,000,000 books for a simple reason: it works.

Available from PuddleDancer Press, the Center for Nonviolent Communication, all major bookstores, and Amazon.com. Distributed by Independent Publisher's Group: 800-888-4741. For Best Pricing Visit: NonviolentCommunication.com

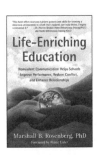

Life-Enriching Education
Nonviolent Communication Helps Schools Improve Performance, Reduce Conflict, and Enhance Relationships
By Marshall B. Rosenberg, PhD

$15.95 — Trade Paper 6x9, 192pp, ISBN: 978-1-892005-05-2

Maximize Every Student's Potential!
Filled with insight, adaptable exercises, and role-plays, gives educators practical skills to generate mutually respectful classroom relationships. Rediscover the joy of teaching in a classroom where each person's needs are respected!

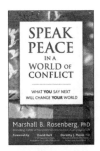

Speak Peace in a World of Conflict
What You Say Next Will Change Your World
By Marshall B. Rosenberg, PhD

$15.95 — Trade Paper 5-3/8x8-3/8, 208pp, ISBN: 978-1-892005-17-5

Create Peace in the Language You Use!
International peacemaker, mediator, and healer, Marshall Rosenberg shows you how the language you use is the key to enriching life.

Raising Children Compassionately
Parenting the Nonviolent Communication Way
By Marshall B. Rosenberg, PhD

$5.95 — Trade Paper 5-3/8x8-3/8, 32pp, ISBN: 978-1-892005-09-0

Learn to create a mutually respectful, enriching family dynamic filled with heartfelt communication.

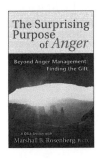

The Surprising Purpose of Anger
Beyond Anger Management: Finding the Gift
By Marshall B. Rosenberg, PhD

$6.95 — Trade Paper 5-3/8x8-3/8, 48pp, ISBN: 978-1-892005-15-1

Marshall shows you how to use anger to discover what you need, and then how to meet your needs in more constructive, healthy ways.

About the Author

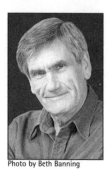

Photo by Beth Banning

Marshall B. Rosenberg, PhD (1934–2015), founded and was for many years the Director of Educational Services for the Center for Nonviolent Communication, an international peacemaking organization.

During his life he authored fifteen books, including the bestselling *Nonviolent Communication: A Language of Life* (PuddleDancer Press), which has sold more than six million copies worldwide and has been translated into more than thirty-five languages, with more translations in the works.

Dr. Rosenberg has received a number of awards for his Nonviolent Communication work including:

2014: Champion of Forgiveness Award from the Worldwide Forgiveness Alliance
2006: Bridge of Peace Nonviolence Award from the Global Village Foundation
2005: Light of God Expressing in Society Award from the Association of Unity Churches
2004: Religious Science International Golden Works Award
2004: International Peace Prayer Day Man of Peace Award by the Healthy, Happy Holy (3HO) Organization
2002: Princess Anne of England and Chief of Police Restorative Justice Appreciation Award
2000: International Listening Association Listener of the Year Award

Dr. Rosenberg first used the NVC process in federally funded school integration projects to provide mediation and communication skills training during the 1960s. The Center for Nonviolent Communication, which he founded in 1984, now has hundreds of certified NVC trainers and supporters teaching NVC in more than sixty countries around the globe.

A sought-after presenter, peacemaker, and visionary leader, Dr. Rosenberg led NVC workshops and international intensive trainings for tens of thousands of people in more than sixty countries around the world and provided training and initiated peace programs in many war-torn areas including Nigeria, Sierra Leone, and the Middle East. He worked tirelessly with educators, managers, health care providers, lawyers, military officers, prisoners, police and prison officials, government officials, and individual families. With guitar and puppets in hand and a spiritual energy that filled a room, Marshall showed us how to create a more peaceful and satisfying world.